JAZZ IS ELEMENTARY

Creativity Development through Music Activities, Movement Games, and Dances, for K–5

DARLA S. HANLEY, ALLISON P. KIPP

FOREWORD BY BASSIST VICTOR WOOTEN

To access online teaching aids and videos visit:
www.halleonard.com/mylibrary

Enter Code
5469-9163-1105-7021

D0905690

BERKLEE PRESS

Editor in Chief: Jonathan Feist
Senior Vice President of Online Learning and Continuing Education/CEO of Berklee Online: Debbie Cavalier
Vice President of Enrollment Marketing and Management: Mike King
Vice President of Academic Strategy: Carin Nuernberg
Editorial Assistant: Brittany McCorriston
Illustrator: Darla S. Hanley

ISBN 978-0-87639-217-2

Berklee
Press

1140 Boylston Street
Boston, MA 02215-3693 USA
(617) 747-2146

Visit Berklee Press Online at
www.berkleepress.com

Berklee Online

Study music online at
online.berklee.edu

DISTRIBUTED BY

HAL•LEONARD®
7777 W. BLUEMOUND RD. P.O. BOX 13819
MILWAUKEE, WISCONSIN 53213

Visit Hal Leonard Online
www.halleonard.com

Berklee Press, a publishing activity of Berklee College of Music, is a not-for-profit educational publisher.
Available proceeds from the sales of our products are contributed to the scholarship funds of the college.

LEAD SHEET (CONTENTS)

APPENDICES

ABOUT THE AUTHORS

ONLINE MATERIALS

Videos

1.10. Blue Skies and Happy Dances

2.9. Pie Pan Partners

3.2. Dixieland Duos

3.6. Howdy Hay Dance

4.4. High Fives in 5

4.6. The Swing Sick Strut Dance

4.7. Plates with Pizzazz

4.9. Streets and Sounds

5.2. We ♥ Dance

5.3. Counting with Cups

5.4. Ritzy Top Hats

Supplementary Information

About *Jazz Is Elementary* Online Materials: A Guide

Artist Profiles

Discography

Visual Aids (Printable)

K.8. Red, Yellow, Blue: Color Cards

K.8. Red, Yellow, Blue: Color Sheets

K.9. Sweepy Moonbeams and Dancing Stars: Moon and Star Visual Aid (Black and White)

K.9. Sweepy Moonbeams and Dancing Stars: Moon and Star Visual Aid (Color)

1.2. Swinging Down the Railroad Tracks: Transportation Visual Aids

1.5. Hittin' the Town: Formal Attire Visual Aid

1.5. Hittin' the Town: Clothing for Settings Visual Aid

1.9. Tea Cups for Two: Tea Cup Iconic Rhythmic Notation Cards

3.4. USA States in Improv: USA State Cards

3.10. Finding Partners: Movement Cards

4.5. Groovin' on the Sunny Side: Small Happy Cards

5.4. Ritzy Top Hats: Color Cards*

5.9. It's in the Bag: Movement Directive Cards

*These are the same color cards as K.8.

ACKNOWLEDGMENTS

From Darla

Inspiration comes from many places. For me, this book is based on years of teaching great students (including my co-author) and conducting workshops for teachers around the world. I appreciate all of the experiences shared and have learned a lot from field-testing pedagogical ideas and exploring new ways to advance music making. Thanks to all of you for following my lead and responding with your full creative self as groovy cats, dancing stars, and so much more. To my co-author, Allison, I thank you for making the process of writing such a joy, and for bringing your voice as a seasoned K–5 music teacher to the project.

Every student is shaped by her teachers. In that lane, I especially thank Ken Almeida, Ruth Ashley, and Edwin Gordon for making me a better musician and educator. Additionally, I recognize my mother, Evelyn, who gave me the inspiration and space to be creative in every conceivable way; and my beloved Jeffrey for his unwavering support in everything I do.

From Allison

I believe there is no greater joy than seeing a child changed by music. This book was inspired by my passion for teaching young musicians, years in the elementary classroom, and a love of jazz music.

To my co-author, Darla, thank you for your friendship, continuing to show me that there are always teachable moments, and for making me a better educator. It has been my pleasure to be by your side and to work together on this project.

To my husband Mike, thank you for being my rock, sharing my love of music, and always reminding me that I can do anything that I put my mind to.

To my son, Lincoln, and daughter, Monroe, thank you for showing me a love that is far greater than myself and for giving me the gift of experiencing the world through the eyes of a child. You inspire me to be the best version of myself, always.

To my parents, Rich and Cheri, who from an early age recognized my love for music and allowed me to pursue every musical endeavor I set out to accomplish; and to my brothers Ricky and Kenny, for giving me the gift of a lifetime—memories of making music together.

Finally, we acknowledge Jonathan Feist and his teams at Berklee Press and Hal Leonard for believing in this project and assisting us with such great guidance and insights.

FOREWORD

By Victor Wooten

Like most people, I began learning how to speak as a baby. Unlike most people, I was also learning to speak the musical language at the same time. I was lucky. My early musical experiences allowed me to freely and musically express myself. Performing with my four older brothers provided me the opportunity to learn to speak with music in the same way and at the same time as I was organically learning how to speak with words. I was allowed to musically express myself in the same way babies are encouraged to express themselves using their own voice. The most important part was that in both languages, I had something to say and my family allowed me to freely speak.

What would happen if all students were introduced to jazz at an early age and encouraged to express themselves through music regardless of whether they were doing it right or wrong? What if young students were allowed to decide for themselves which notes were right or wrong? What if we were encouraged to create *before* we learned all the rules? I'll answer for you. We would have a world of amateur and professional musicians who are confident, who are not afraid to improvise, play in front of others, make mistakes, compose, jam, and again... improvise. That is beautiful! Jazz embodies all of these elements in an extremely impactful way. Studies have already shown that the addition of music in early education helps children grow to be more confident and self-assured. Music also helps us learn and understand the important benefits of listening as well as speaking. That is why I'm convinced that all students should be exposed to jazz at an early age. That is also one of the reasons why I'm so excited about this book.

Within these pages you will find a collection of original games, dances, and activities using authentic jazz recordings that are connected to iconic jazz artists. These teaching strategies, along with a curated audio playlist which you can augment with your students, are intended to help foster creativity and improvisation in both teachers and students. This early exposure is invaluable. Parents, teachers, students, homeschoolers, adventurers, and those of us who just want to grow and/or help others grow, this book is for us. Allow it to help you express new ways to experience the joys of being creative.

Jazz Is Elementary is intended to be used as a process, a springboard for further exploration, and a collection of enriching activities (reminiscent of how I grew up). This is truly a book that can benefit the world. Allow it to inspire! Read it! Digest it! Live it! Share it! Repeat! Trust me! The process works. I thank the authors for this great work. I thank you, the readers, for bringing it to life.

—**Victor L. Wooten**
(Multi-Grammy winning musician, composer, writer, and educator)

Calling the Tune:
Pedagogical Foundations

INTRODUCING JAZZ

Jazz is an American artform built on personal expression, interpretation, improvisation, and style. It is rooted in the African American experience and is filled with emotion—helping us tell stories and connect. Further, the evolution of jazz from its beginnings in the early 20th century until today illustrates a blending of people, thoughts, culture, history, creativity, boundary pushing, and artistry.

Jazz includes distinctive features like syncopated rhythms and swing, riffs, harmonic progressions, articulations, blue notes, and vocabulary—providing musicians with space to create spontaneously and interact with each other in the moment to make art. Jazz musicians share musical conversations as they shape melodies, trade solos, and support each other with chord changes and accompaniments during live performance. Together they make music that is defined by a groove, a feel, and a spirit. The result is a fresh and engaging musical style that captivates those who have the ability to make jazz as well as those who have the opportunity to experience the jazz created by others.

There are many kinds of jazz ranging from big band swing, to be-bop, hard-bop, a cappella, fusion, and free jazz. In several cases, these types of jazz can be attributed to specific artists offering their original voice to the artform. Artists like Louis Armstrong, Ella Fitzgerald, Dave Brubeck, Thelonious Monk, Sarah Vaughan, Miles Davis, and Duke Ellington exemplify this idea and are historical jazz legends whose musical offerings have stood the test of time. Today, artists like Victor Wooten, Bria Skonberg, and Hiromi are advancing jazz with audiences all around the world—continuing jazz traditions and blurring lines to take this music in new directions.

As we consider the future of jazz music, it's critical to recognize the importance of young audiences experiencing and knowing its history and foundations, and planting the seed that these children are quite possibly jazz giants or jazz patrons of tomorrow.

WHY JAZZ IN K–5 GENERAL MUSIC

Music teachers teach what they know and value. They make decisions regarding curriculum, learning experiences, instructional modalities, and examples/repertoire to present in their classrooms every day. They shape the education offered to students and in turn, shape what students know and are able to do (independently). This means that it is essential for music teachers to know and bring a variety of high-quality musical examples, across styles and genres, into their work—including jazz.

The creative nature of jazz music is perfect for the elementary classroom. The goal of this book is to provide a resource that guides teachers to use this music and engage young learners to be creative. Note: This book is not intended to be a curriculum or method; rather we offer a collection of creative teaching strategies to promote jazz-inspired music teaching and learning in the K–5 classroom.

Elementary music instruction is primarily centered around singing, playing, listening, and moving. These learning targets are typically experienced through informal and formal exposure to children's songs and musical styles such as classical and folk music along with poems, stories, and chants. Jazz music can also be used to advance these targets.

We all know that elementary education provides a foundation for all future learning—across academic and artistic disciplines. Accordingly, it is important for children to begin hearing the sounds of jazz in the elementary music classroom, and for music teachers to share its history and style as part of compelling K–5 learning experiences. Children are often transformed when they hear powerful and moving (jazz) music in conjunction with opportunities for participation, creativity, and expression.

Jazz music is essential in the elementary classroom because it enhances critical listening skills, sparks imaginations, and provides an outlet for spontaneous musical choices. Further, it fosters a setting to express preferences and opinions, and develops critical and creative thinkers.

CREATIVITY AND IMPROVISATION IN MUSIC

The need for creativity is important more than ever in our fast-paced world, and the music classroom is the perfect place to engage students and provide space for them to imagine, express, and experience. By fostering creativity and improvisation in the music classroom we are allowing students to "be kids" and explore the musical world around them through sounds and play. The more creative opportunities we provide for students, the more creative they will become. Additionally, it is important for teachers to establish a safe educational environment to support creative risk-taking where students will have the ability to gain confidence and find their own voice.

Jazz music showcases one of the greatest forms of creative expression—improvisation. Improvisation fosters self-expression and allows application and connection of musical concepts through personal interpretation. Ultimately, improvisation is music making based on musical choice and allows students to respond, create, and perform within a spontaneous context.

Improvisation in elementary music can take the simplest form: speaking nonsense syllables within a chant, offering original ideas for movements based on a musical prompt or lyrical content, exploring ways to play instruments, or having "musical conversations" where students take turns spontaneously. It can be as complex as vocal improvisation with scat syllables, moving to show the feeling of a piece, reflecting jazz style using personal preferences, or making musical decisions to create on the spot with instruments, voices, and/or movement.

Accordingly, throughout this book, you will find a collection of original jazz-based teaching strategies that inspire students to meet learning outcomes in Respond, Create, and Perform categories—with singing, instrument play, and movement. The strategies are designed to foster creativity and imagination and provide a context for students to experience jazz and the joys of music making.

JAZZ IS ELEMENTARY DISTINCTIVE ELEMENTS

There are several features of this book that are strategically designed to help you implement the teaching strategies and foster creativity and improvisation. The following is a description of those elements.

 ### Set the Stage

The educational stage is set when teachers create learning environments that are welcoming, safe, and rich with opportunities for students to explore, experience, and grow. These settings contribute to prepare students for success and inspire creativity.

Best educational practices also set the stage for learning when we offer context, create developmentally appropriate opportunities for individuals and groups, and reinforce vocabulary, for example. Accordingly, within the teaching strategies, you will find scripted text (in italics) as suggested ways of framing directions, content, and questions; and recommended vocabulary words to emphasize (shown in bold font).

Additionally, throughout this book you will find "set the stage" elements that provide ideas for creating a learning environment "scene" and/or enhancing the musical experience with themed bulletin boards, discussion prompts, games, and visual aids.

Learning Targets

Each teaching strategy includes a section showing learning outcomes and targets. As previously mentioned, learning outcomes are provided within Respond, Create, and Perform categories. Learning targets are offered to show the specific foci for the strategy in terms of the following experiences for students: arrange, compose, connect, describe, improvise, imitate, lead, listen, move, play, read, and sing. An overview of learning target applications is provided as an appendix to help you identify specific targets addressed across all sixty teaching strategies (see page 136).

Cues

Cues are offered within each teaching strategy to share tips and best practices that are designed to help advance the learning experience and communicate suggestions. These are the kinds of things teachers share with each other based on professional experience in the classroom, and we are happy to include them for you.

 ## Riffs

Within the teaching strategies, you will find numerous opportunities to extend the learning experiences with ideas offered as "riffs." These ideas include new ways to expand the strategy by adding tracks, artists, and/or jazz styles; playing different instruments; working in partners; creating or changing dance steps; and more. Additionally, riffs are designed to engage students with experiences that are familiar yet different, and enhance their developing skills and knowledge.

 ## Take a Solo

Assessment is an essential part of teaching and learning and happens in many ways. Throughout this book you will find opportunities to *informally assess* students as they sing, play, move, improvise, and create. These formative assessment opportunities are designed to connect with national and state educational standards.

Additionally, we offer "take a solo" opportunities for students to individually demonstrate developing skills and knowledge, leadership, and original expressions. These "solos" are structured to authentically connect to the jazz music, learning targets, and the developmental level of students by grade.

Finally, we designed learning experiences within the strategies that adhere to the following six assessment principles:

1. Set clear goals that support music making and creativity.
2. Provide opportunities for students to show what they know and build on prior learning.
3. Provide opportunities for students to reflect and self-evaluate.
4. Structure assessment experiences that are developmentally creative and playful while advancing knowledge/skills and application.
5. Carefully choose language and offer feedback for students that is constructive, clear, and meaningful.
6. Include both formative and summative assessments to routinely (informally) observe students and (formally) track/document individuals.

ARTIST PROFILES

Each artist has a story—a life filled with experiences that shape who they are and the music they make. We included Artist Profiles as an online PDF to provide biographical details, "note-able" accomplishments, and context as baseline information for you to get to know the artists included in our teaching strategies.

Note: These profiles are not intended to be lecture-type content for students; rather, they are offered as a companion resource for teachers to inform instruction. These profiles only begin to tell their stories. We recommend that you expand this information to know more about the artists and their music, to further inform students about jazz within history and American culture.

Jazz, like most music, is made when people collaborate. Accordingly, the artist profiles also illustrate an historic arc of the jazz community showing musicians coming together across the USA and beyond, and in venues, studios, and clubs to create original offerings and push artistic boundaries.

STREAMING AUDIO IN THE ELEMENTARY MUSIC CLASSROOM

Today, the world of music is literally in our hands. With technological advances like streaming audio, everyone (including children) is able to listen to a variety of music any time of day.

Streaming audio platforms offer millions of tracks representing music across decades of people, place, and time. This vast resource provides a seemingly limitless bounty of examples to be used in the music classroom and beyond.

If we pause for a moment and reflect, it's pretty clear that music is all around us. It's on television and film, in the supermarket, in elevators, taxicabs, places of worship, schools, and of course, in concert halls and other music venues. There is so much music in our world that it may seem like a natural soundtrack to life—something that is always present and heard; however, with such a firehose of sound around us it may be possible that children no longer experience targeted and strategic music listening to essential artforms, like jazz. Further, without formal exposure, children may never know that much of the music they hear in those movies and restaurants actually is jazz.

In past generations, children primarily heard the music played by or selected by their parents or caregivers at home, in their community, and in school. The adults made musical choices based on their personal preferences, what society was defining as the popular music of the day, or music that stood the test of time (i.e., classics, masterworks, renowned artists and composers). In school, music teachers previously relied upon recordings associated with textbooks or music they personally owned and brought into the classroom. Streaming audio has completely changed the game.

Streaming audio provides music teachers with the ability to expand the repertoire shared with children and blur lines between music in society and music in a school setting. With this tool, we are able to bring an ever-evolving menu of music into the classroom. Further, streaming audio allows us to target particular styles of music, like jazz, and introduce it to new audiences.

Playlist

This book is driven by a curated playlist of jazz music that is available on many streaming audio platforms. After years of work with *Spotify* and with classroom teachers (across disciplines across the United States), the authors of this book learned that one of the biggest challenges teachers face when using streaming audio to enhance instruction is identifying examples. This book is designed to do that for you. We selected nearly eighty renowned jazz artists to inspire teachers to not only use these specific examples, but also to serve as prompts for further discovery of tracks by these people and/or within the fabulous world of jazz music.

The playlist was carefully crafted to offer examples across jazz styles and support innovative K–5 learning experiences. We selected specific recordings/performances for the strategies and recognize that you may find other versions of these tunes. (Note: Timings, when offered, are approximations that match the recordings we used. They may differ among versions.) We recommend that you use this playlist as an introduction to the artists and take time to research them to identify additional examples for use with students. Further, once new tracks are identified, we recommend that you create your own playlists to maintain and organize an ever-growing selection of music to inspire teaching and learning (and share them with other music teacher colleagues).

TAG: FINAL THOUGHTS

This book was written to advance music education and share jazz with K–5 learners. The teaching strategies offered illustrate frameworks and learning experiences that may be adapted and expanded for use in a variety of teaching settings. We recommend that you apply the teaching strategies to see what resonates in your classroom and continue to build opportunities for students to experience jazz.

We wish you rewarding teaching and engaged students as you implement the teaching strategies and introduce jazz to K–5 students. You're never too young for jazz.... *Jazz Is Elementary!*

ADDITIONAL MATERIALS ONLINE

To access the accompanying videos and PDFs, go to www.halleonard.com/mylibrary and enter the code found on the first page of this book. This will grant you access to a variety of printable resources, a discography, and artist information, as well as instructional videos for selected dances/movement games in the book. Associated online materials are indicated with these icons:

 Video

 Download

See the table of contents (page iii) for a list of the online resources.

Grade K

Kindergarten music is all about exploration.

Kindergarten learning focuses on students experiencing, making, and responding. In music class they listen and share as they build vocabulary, offer original ideas, and begin to formally sing and play instruments in a group setting.

Kindergarten musical experiences should include a variety of activities, allowing students to explore the elements of classroom music while promoting self-expression and participation. Additionally, these experiences need to be fast-paced with well-executed transitions to maximize learning. Assessment at the kindergarten level should be formative, informally observing and documenting notable participation rather than mastery of musical skill.

Fundamentally, kindergarten music lessons include singing, playing, moving and listening—with lots of opportunity for informal exposure and play. In terms of jazz, kindergarten is the perfect setting to begin exposing students to this American artform—engaging them to imitate, respond, perform, and create in conjunction with iconic and exemplary artists and examples.

At the kindergarten level, the jazz-based teaching strategies presented in this book will engage students to respond, create, and perform, in the following ways.

LEARNING OUTCOMES
Respond

- Demonstrate steady beat (macrobeat and/or microbeat).
- Employ non-locomotor and/or locomotor movement.
- Explore uses of the voice.
- Express ideas verbally.
- Express personal preferences with rationale.
- Imitate musical sounds and concepts.
- Move to reflect style of music.
- Move to show macrobeat and microbeat.
- Use instruments or singing voice to express ideas.

Create

- Create personal interpretations.
- Create scat/nonsense syllables.
- Explore new ways to play instruments and/or use the voice.
- Offer ideas for non-locomotor and/or locomotor movement.

Perform

- Perform chants, play-party games, stories, and/or poems with music.
- Perform individually.
- Perform original non-locomotor and/or locomotor movement.
- Perform rhythmic patterns.
- Perform simple body percussion.
- Perform with a partner.
- Play classroom percussion instruments.
- Sing simple songs, melodic patterns, and/or melodies.
- Use manipulative/prop to depict a musical idea.

K.1. Groovy Cat Moves/Scoobie Doobie Swim Moves: Movement Exploration

Learning Outcomes

Respond:
- Employ non-locomotor and/or locomotor movement.
- Move to reflect style of music.
- Move to show macrobeat and microbeat.

Create:
- Create personal interpretations.
- Offer ideas for non-locomotor and/or locomotor movement.

Perform:
- Perform original non-locomotor and/or locomotor movement.

Learning Targets
✓Listen ✓Move

Music Selections
- "Everybody Wants to Be a Cat" Roy Hargrove (*Disney Jazz Volume 1: Everybody Wants to Be a Cat*, Disney Pearl, 2011)
- "Soul Bossa Nova" Quincy Jones (*Big Band Bossa Nova*, Verve, 1962)

Setup/Materials
- Space for movement

Teaching Strategy

1. Play the recording of "Everybody Wants to Be a Cat." Ask students to copy your moves to feel the style and beat of the music.

2. *The name of this song is "Everybody Wants to Be a Cat," so let's pretend we are groovy cats prowling around to this jazz music.* Include a variety of groovy cat movements, such as:

NON-LOCOMOTOR OR LOCOMOTOR	LOCOMOTOR
cat paw hands	prowling cat feet
head nod ("yes" to the beat)	prowling cat feet with cat paw hands
head sway (left right, single and/or double)	
stretching like a cat	

 Riff: Invite students to pretend to be jazz fish and perform scoobie-doobie swim movements with the recording such as:

NON-LOCOMOTOR OR LOCOMOTOR	LOCOMOTOR
splashing movements flicking pretend water	walking and pretending to be a fish swimming in water
swimming arms (two hands in front of body)	
swimming arms (one arm at a time above head)	
splashing movements flicking pretend water	

 Riff: To vary the learning experience, play the recording of "Soul Bossa Nova," and repeat the movement exploration.

K.2. Steady Ricky: Steady Beat

Learning Outcomes

Respond:

- Demonstrate steady beat (macrobeat and/or microbeat).
- Explore uses of the voice.
- Imitate musical sounds and concepts.

Create:

- Create personal interpretations.
- Explore new ways to play instruments and/or use the voice.

Perform:

- Perform rhythmic patterns.
- Play classroom percussion instruments.

Learning Targets

✓Describe ✓Imitate ✓Lead ✓Listen ✓Play

Music Selections

- "Song for My Father" Horace Silver (*Blue Note 101: A Jazz Introduction*, CM Blue Note [A92], 2014)
- "Song for My Father" Victor Wooten (*Palmystery*, Vix Records, 2008)

Setup/Materials

- Rhythm sticks

 Set the Stage: Create color sheets with musical contrasts (e.g., images depicting high/low, fast/slow, loud/soft) for students to color, and post them in the music room.

Teaching Strategy

1. Play the recording, and ask students to chant "Steady Ricky" (Ta-di, Ta-di) with the track.

> ## Cue
> This is an opportunity to introduce dynamics by chanting "Steady Ricky" at *p*, *mf*, and *f* levels and varying vocal timbres by chanting with a **high** voice/**low** voice for students to copy. Encourage students to listen closely and "do what you do."

2. Speaking in a high voice: *Raise your hand if you think this is my high voice.* (Yes) *How did you know?*

3. Speaking in a low voice: *Raise your hand if you think this is my low voice.* (Yes) *How did you know?*

4. Ask students to chant "Steady Ricky" (Ta-di, Ta-di) with their high or low voice as called by the teacher. *Listen carefully, so you know which voice to use.*

5. Distribute **rhythm sticks** (two per child), and inform/remind students of the name of this instrument and how to hold and play it.

6. Show two ways of playing—tapping sticks together, tapping sticks on the floor—and lead students to play the **steady beat** using both ways.

7. *Now we are going to listen to jazz music called "Song for My Father" by Horace Silver, and play our instruments with the recording.* Play the recording, and ask students to copy the manner in which you play the "Steady Ricky" with the track.

8. **Take a Solo:** Ask a student to decide which way to play (i.e., together or on the floor), play the recording, and guide everyone to play following the student's lead.

   Riff: Insert other two-syllable names to replace "Ricky" including names of students in the room, or in this case, "Steady Horace" to mention the artist.

   Riff: Play the Victor Wooten recording of "Song for My Father," and ask students to move or play rhythm sticks while chanting, "Steady Victor."

> ## Cue
> The tempo of the Victor Wooten version is faster than the Horace Silver track. Additionally, the first 1:22 of the track and/or 4:20 to the end provide the clearest straightforward pulse for kindergarten learners.

K.3. Tap It, Twist It, Wave: Movement with Partners

Learning Outcomes

Respond:

- Demonstrate steady beat (macrobeat and/or microbeat).
- Employ non-locomotor and/or locomotor movement.
- Imitate musical sounds and concepts.

Create:

- Create personal interpretations.

Perform:

- Perform original non-locomotor and/or locomotor movement.
- Perform rhythmic patterns.
- Perform with a partner.

Learning Targets

✓Listen ✓Move ✓Sing

Music Selection

- "Black Orpheus" (Manhã de Carnaval) Quincy Jones (*Big Band Bossa Nova*, Verve, 1962)

Setup/Materials

- Seated in a circle on the floor

Teaching Strategy

1. Sing a familiar song, and ask students to demonstrate a way to tap the **steady beat** while they sing. Guide them to patsching.

> ## Cue
> By singing a familiar song, students are reinforcing prior learning while focusing on/ demonstrating original ways to tap the steady beat.

2. Play the recording of "Black Orpheus," and ask students to speak the words, "tap, tap, tap, tap" as they patsch (macrobeat).

3. Show a twisting movement with torso/hips, and ask students to speak the words, "twist, twist, twist, twist" as they move (macrobeat). Play the recording, and twist to the steady beat.

4. Ask students to wave their hands and speak the words "wave, wave, wave, wave" as they move (macrobeat). Play the recording, and lead movement.

5. *Now we will put all three of our movements together. We will tap and twist and wave. Watch and listen closely to copy movements and find the beat.* Play the recording, and perform the pattern with words and movements.

Patsch: **Twist Torso:**   **Wave:**

| Tap | Tap | Tap | Tap | Twist | Twist | Twist | Twist | Wave | Wave | Wave | Wave |
| Ta | Ta | Ta | Ta | Ta | Ta | Ta | Ta | Ta | Ta | Ta | Ta |

FIG. K.3. Tap It, Twist It, Wave Movement Sequence

6. Guide students to find a partner. *Be sure to speak the words as you move, and look at your partner to see if you are moving in the same way and both finding the beat.* Play the recording, and perform the movements.

> ## Cue
> Ask students to whisper the words as they move to anchor the rhythm/movement pattern and keep the recording audible by everyone.

 Riff: Ask partners to stand and perform movements with the recording.

Riff—Take a Solo: Ask students to identify new ways to tap, twist, and/or wave.

K.4. Pretty Jazz Music to Dance With: Scarf Dance

Learning Outcomes

Respond:

- Demonstrate steady beat (macrobeat and/or microbeat).
- Employ non-locomotor and/or locomotor movement.
- Move to reflect style of music.

Create:

- Create personal interpretations.

Perform:

- Perform original non-locomotor and/or locomotor movement.
- Use manipulative/prop to depict a musical idea.

Learning Targets

✓Listen ✓Move

Music Selections

- "I Hear Music" Blossom Dearie (*Blossom Dearie [Expanded Edition]*, Verve Reissues, 1957)
- "Seeker" Hiromi Uehara (*Alive*, Telarc, 2014)

Setup/Materials

- Space for movement; scarves

Teaching Strategy

1. Distribute scarves (one per student).

   Riff: Use streamers or ribbons if scarves are unavailable, or instead of scarves, to vary the learning experience.

2. *Now we are going to listen to a song by a jazz singer named Blossom Dearie called, "I Hear Music."* Play the recording, and ask students to make their scarf dance to the music (non-locomotor).

   > ## Cue
   >
   > Demonstrate a variety of ways to make the scarf move (i.e., bounce, float, twirl, lasso) to prompt students, as needed.

3. *Now let's make our scarf bounce to the **steady beat** of the music as we listen and speak, "I Hear Mu-sic, I Hear Mu-sic"* (i.e., the macrobeat: Ta, Ta, Ta, Ta).

   Riff: Invite students to make their scarves dance to the music around the room (locomotor).

4. Lead a "Start and Stop" scarf dance pausing the track to inform students to stop when the sound stops and move when the music is playing (non-locomotor or locomotor).

   Riff: Repeat using Hiromi's recording of "Seeker," asking students to bounce scarves to the microbeat.

   > ## Cue
   >
   > The first 0:58 of the track by Hiromi emphasizes the microbeat.

K.5. Pass the Scat Hat: Scat Patterns

Learning Outcomes

Respond:

- Imitate musical sounds and concepts.
- Use instruments or singing voice to express ideas.

Create:

- Create scat/nonsense syllables.

Perform:

- Perform chants, play-party games, stories, and/or poems with music.
- Perform individually.
- Sing simple songs, melodic patterns, and/or melodies.

Learning Targets

✓Improvise ✓Imitate ✓Listen ✓Sing

Music and Chant Selections

- "The Scat Hat" Allison P. Kipp
- "Bye, Bye Blackbird" Clark Terry and Bobby Brookmeyer (*Gingerbread*, Mainstream Records, 1991)
- "Bye, Bye Blackbird" The Red Garland Trio (*At the Prelude*, Prestige, 2006)

Setup/Materials

- Seated in a circle; glitter top hat

Teaching Strategy

1. *Today, we will be speaking in a musical language called **scat**. We will use nonsense words, and our classmates will echo our words.*

2. Demonstrate the chant, and ask students to raise their hand when they hear scat syllables

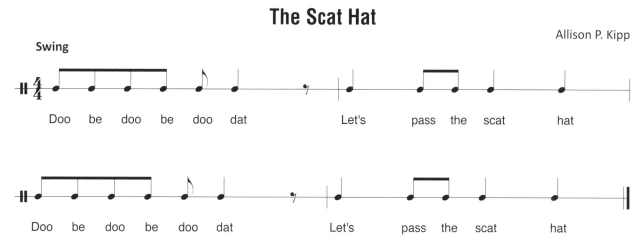

FIG. K.5. The Scat Hat Chant

3. Teach "The Scat Hat" by rote (whole-part-whole), and repeat until the chant becomes familiar to the students.

4. **Take a Solo:** Add the top hat and instruct students that they will pass it around the circle during the chant, and when the chant ends the person holding the hat creates an original scat phrase.

> ## Cues
> - Demonstrate four-beat scat patterns to provide examples for students. Display a list of scat syllables on the board to guide students as they create their own scat phrase.
> - Practice passing the hat around the circle before performing the chant with the hat.
> - The goal is for students to explore and imitate scat syllables, not perform in rhythm or meter.

5. Play the Clark Terry or Red Garland track of "Bye, Bye Blackbird," and have students perform the scat patterns with a recording.

> ## Cue
> The Red Garland track is a live recording, which provides an opportunity to talk about live performance and when to applaud in jazz music. Typically, applause occurs after solos and at the conclusion.

Riff: Ask students to sing the chant on Sol and Mi and perform their original scat phrase using those pitches.

K.6. Tappin' Toes: Rhythmic Ostinato

Learning Outcomes

Respond:

- Demonstrate steady beat (macrobeat and/or microbeat).
- Employ non-locomotor and/or locomotor movement.
- Imitate musical sounds and concepts.

Create:

- Offer ideas for non-locomotor and/or locomotor movement.

Perform:

- Perform rhythmic patterns.
- Perform simple body percussion.
- Play classroom percussion instruments.

Learning Targets

✓Describe ✓Imitate ✓Move ✓Play

Music Selection

- "Just Swinging" Tommy Dorsey (*Tommy Dorsey King of Swing*, Wnts, 2011)

Setup/Materials

- Drums, shakers

Teaching Strategy

1. Play the recording of "Just Swinging" by Tommy Dorsey and have students imitate movements such as: tap, stomp, pat, and clap to the steady beat.

2. Invite students to speak and clap the following "tappin' toes" pattern:
   Tappin' Toes, Tappin' Toes
   [Ta - di Ta,   Ta - di Ta]

3. *How else can we perform the "tappin' toes" pattern?* (patting shoulders, stomping feet, etc.)

> ### Cue
> Demonstrate a variety of ways to perform the pattern using body percussion if students need a prompt.

4. **Take a Solo:** Invite individual students to perform the pattern using body percussion of their choice.

5. *Let's perform our tappin' toes pattern with the music!* Play the recording, and guide students to move to show the "tappin' toes" pattern.

6. Divide the class into two groups (Group 1 = Drums; Group 2 = Shakers) and distribute instruments. Play the recording, and lead groups in a "point-and-play" back and forth performing the "tappin' toes" pattern in turn.

   Riff: Ask students to trade instruments and perform the "tappin' toes" pattern with the recording.

> ### Cue
> This learning experience provides an opportunity for students to demonstrate the ability to follow directions, non-verbal cues, and self-control.

7. Lead a discussion to engage students to reflect on their participation. *How did you know when it was your turn to play?*

K.7. Lullaby My Jazzy Baby: Movement Exploration

Learning Outcomes

Respond:

- Employ non-locomotor and/or locomotor movement.
- Express personal preferences with rationale.
- Move to reflect style of music.

Create:

- Create personal interpretations.

Perform:

- Perform original non-locomotor and/or locomotor movement.

Learning Targets

✓Connect ✓Describe ✓Imitate ✓Listen ✓Move

Music Selections

- "Hit the Road to Dreamland" Mel Tormé, the Meltones (*Jazz Lullaby*, Verve Reissues, 2008)
- "Little Child (Daddy Dear)" Wes Montgomery (*Jazz Lullaby*, Verve Reissues, 2008)
- "Theme for Ernie" John Coltrane (*Coltrane '58: The Prestige Recordings*, Craft Recordings, 2019)

Setup/Materials

- Space for movement

Teaching Strategy

1. Play the recording of "Hit the Road to Dreamland," and ask students to copy movements to feel the style of the music. Include a variety of sleepy/lullaby movements such as:

NON-LOCOMOTOR
pretend to hold a baby in your arms and sway to the music
head nod ("yes" to the beat)
stretch (like we just woke up)

2. Demonstrate arms moving and swaying to show a "rock a pretend baby to sleep" action. *What are we trying to do when we rock a baby like this?* (Get them to fall asleep, calm them.)

3. *We call gentle, quiet music that soothes us to sleep a **lullaby**. Raise your hand if you ever listen to lullaby music when you are getting ready to fall asleep.*

4. *Let's stand up and tiptoe quietly around the room to this jazz music—pretending there is a sleeping baby nearby. Watch closely to know how to move.*

LOCOMOTOR
tip-toe
tip-toe with "praying sleep hands with head tilted"

> ## Cue
>
> Model swaying (freely) in response to the music as well as to the pulse for students to copy. The focus is on eliciting a movement response that matches the sounds.

Riff: Ask students to perform movements with the recording of "Little Child (Daddy Dear)" or "Theme for Ernie" such as:

NON-LOCOMOTOR OR LOCOMOTOR	LOCOMOTOR
holding a pretend baby and gently rocking it to the beat	walking and pretending to sleepwalk to the beat with arms stretched out in front of body

5. *Which music did you like best to help the baby go to sleep? What did you like about it?*

> ## Cue
>
> Asking students to share personal preferences with a rationale provides an opportunity to foster decision making skills.

K.8. Red, Yellow, Blue: Color Arrangements

Learning Outcomes

Respond:

- Express ideas verbally.
- Imitate musical sounds and concepts.
- Use instruments or singing voice to express ideas.

Create:

- Create personal interpretations.

Perform:

- Perform chants, play-party games, stories, and/or poems with music.
- Perform individually.
- Sing simple songs, melodic patterns, and/or melodies.

Learning Targets

✓Arrange ✓Connect ✓Lead ✓Listen ✓Move ✓Sing

Music and Chant Selections

- "Red Top" Les McCann (*Talkin' Verve*, Verve, 1998)
- "Red, Yellow, Blue" Darla S. Hanley
- "Red, Yellow, Blue in the Bag" Darla S. Hanley

Setup/Materials

 Seated in a circle; (optional: color sheets or color cards), bag of colored discs

 Set the Stage: Invite students to play a game of "I Spy with My Little Eye" to find colors of objects in the music room.

Teaching Strategy

1. Ask students to listen as you speak the "Red, Yellow, Blue" chant. *Now we are going to play a game. When it is your turn, name a color for everyone to speak four times in a row.*

Red, Yellow, Blue

Darla S. Hanley

Red, yellow, blue

This is what to do

Name a color when I point to you

 2. **Take a Solo:** Perform the chant, and lead the game inviting individual students to name a color followed by everyone speaking it four times.

3. *We are going to play the game with jazz music called "Red Top" by an artist named Les McCann.* Play the recording, and perform the game.

> **Cue**
>
> Insert "groove breaks" in between chants to add space for students to move to reflect the sounds of the music and prepare for their turn.

4. Create a class "color arrangement" by identifying four color names and putting them in a sequence. Play the recording of "Red Top," and invite students to chant the colors in this order with the track. Identify new sequences of colors to create new arrangements and repeat.

Cue

Have students complete color sheets (e.g., Red with apple; Yellow with sun) or display color cards showing colors to provide a visual element to prompt arrangements.

Riff: Create a "Red, Yellow, Blue" Sol, Mi song or singing game, and ask students to sing colors.

Riff: Invite students to perform the "Red, Yellow, Blue in the Bag" chant.

Red, Yellow, Blue in the Bag

Darla S. Hanley

Red, yellow, blue

This is what to do

Take a color and sing it too

Riff—Take a Solo: Ask students to draw a colored disc (or other clearly single-colored item) from a bag. *This game is like the one we played, but this time you need to draw something from the bag, name its color, and then sing its name.*

Cues

-   Demonstrate the student response by singing the name of a color on a Sol, Do pattern with the words, "It's INSERT COLOR" (e.g., It's blue).

-   Sing with students if they are unable to initially perform the response as an echo. Additionally, use this approach to provide clear expectations and guidance toward solo singing:

    1. Teacher sings the color.

    2. Teacher and student sing the color.

    3. Student sings the color alone.

K.9. Sweepy Moonbeams and Dancing Stars: Movement Exploration

Learning Outcomes

Respond:
- Employ non-locomotor and/or locomotor movement.
- Express personal preferences with rationale.
- Move to reflect style of music.

Create:
- Create personal interpretations.
- Offer ideas for non-locomotor and/or locomotor movement.

Perform:
- Perform original non-locomotor and/or locomotor movement.

Learning Targets

✓Describe ✓Improvise ✓Imitate ✓Listen ✓Move

Music Selections

- "Moonlight Serenade" Glenn Miller (*Ultimate Big Band Collection: Glenn Miller*, Masterworks Jazz, 1939)
- "Blue Moon" Jo Stafford, the Pied Pipers, and the Paul Weston Orchestra (*Isn't It Romantic: The Rodgers and Hart Songbook*, Readers Digest Music, 2013)
- "Fly Me to the Moon" Frank Sinatra and Count Basie (*The Post COVID-19 Mixtape – Love Edition*, Remastered UMG Recordings, Inc., 2015)
- "I Wished on the Moon" Billie Holiday (*The Complete Billie Holiday on Verve 1945–1959*, Verve Reissues, 1992)

Setup/Materials

- Space for movement; pictures of a moon and star

 Set the Stage: Show a picture of a moon and a star, and ask students to raise their hand to name them.

Teaching Strategy

1. Play the recording of "Moonlight Serenade," and ask students to stand and imitate movements (e.g., patsch, sway, bend knees) to feel the style and beat of the music.

2. *Let's pretend to be sweepy moonbeams moving to this jazz music.* Include a variety of moonbeam movements such as:

NON-LOCOMOTOR
rollercoaster arms
head nod ("yes" to the beat)
single arm "half moon" over head

3. Play the recording, and ask students to create sweepy moonbeam movements with the track.

4. *Let's have a sweepy moonbeam parade!* Guide students to form a line (in a follow-the-leader style) and follow you around the room. *Watch closely to know how to move. We need to make sure our sweepy moonbeam parade looks like how the music sounds.*

5. Play the recording of "Moonlight Serenade," and lead the parade.

LOCOMOTOR
walking with wavy arms to the sides
walking with stretching arms over head

Riff: Perform sweepy moonbeam movements (non-locomotor and locomotor) with the recording of "Blue Moon" by Jo Stafford.

6. *Now we are going to pretend to be dancing stars. Listen to this music, and watch closely to know how to move.* Include a variety of star movements such as:

NON-LOCOMOTOR
waving jazz hands
blinking jazz hands

7. *Let's have a dancing star **freestyle**! A freestyle means you can move any way you want to move to show the sounds of the music and be a dancing star. You can stay in place or move around the room. Listen closely and let the music lead your dancing star.*

8. Play the recording of "Fly Me to the Moon" by Frank Sinatra, and guide students to create movements.

Cues

- Asking students to create without providing a specific movement for them to copy may be difficult at this age unless students have previously experienced creative movement. See what happens, and provide movement suggestions, as needed.

- Observe movements and call out cool ideas being performed by individuals (e.g., *Look at how Lincoln is moving… Let's all move like Lincoln's dancing star*). Alternate between all students creating original dancing star moves at the same time and performing movements created by individual students.

Riff: Repeat the dancing star movements (non-locomotor and locomotor) with the recording of "I Wished on the Moon" by Billie Holiday.

9. *Today, we pretended to be sweepy moonbeams and dancing stars. Which did you like best? How did you decide?*

K.10. Sounds Around Us: Word Chains

Learning Outcomes

Respond:
- Demonstrate steady beat (macrobeat and/or microbeat).
- Express ideas verbally.

Create:
- Create personal interpretations.
- Explore new ways to play instruments and/or use the voice.

Perform:
- Perform chants, play-party games, stories, and/or poems with music.
- Perform rhythmic patterns.
- Perform simple body percussion.

Learning Targets

✓Connect ✓Describe ✓Listen ✓Move ✓Play

Music and Chant Selections
- "Come Rain or Come Shine" John Coltrane (*The Last Trane*, Prestige, 1965)
- "Found Sound Safari" Darla S. Hanley

Setup/Materials
- Pen, notebook/technology; (optional: unpitched percussion instruments)

 Set the Stage: Create a "Sounds Around Us" bulletin board that includes images of sounds in nature, found sounds, and instruments.

Teaching Strategy

1. Ask students to listen as you perform the "Found Sound Safari" chant.

Found Sound Safari
Darla S. Hanley

Let's take a trip
A very special trip
A found sound safari
Would be so hip

What will we hear?
What will we find?
A found sound safari
Is on my mind

School bells ringing
Children singing
Games at recess
Make me skip

Let's take a trip
A very special trip
A found sound safari
Would be so hip

2. *We will go on a Found Sound Safari around the school and make a list of sounds we hear to use in a game when we return to the music room. Based on the chant and what you know about our school, what do you think we will hear on our safari?*

3. Guide students to take a walk around the school building to identify both recurring sounds (e.g., ticking clock) and spontaneous sounds (e.g., delivery truck backing up outside), and make a list of sounds identified by students during the safari.

> ## Cue
> Bring a pen and notebook or use technology to document found sounds during the safari.

4. Create a **word chain** using the found sounds identified during the safari, and have students chant the chain.

> ## Cue
> Asking students to select found sounds to create the chain gives them ownership. Use the melodic rhythm of the words as the basis of the chant (e.g., ticking clock—Ta, Ta, Ta, Rest).

5. *Now we are going to learn about a giant of jazz named John Coltrane. Let's listen to him playing a song called "Come Rain or Come Shine," and keep the steady beat. Since this song is about rain and sunshine, let's pretend we are raindrops or flickering rays of sun as we show the steady beat of this music.*

> ## Cue
> This is an opportunity for students to demonstrate steady beat any way they choose. You may need to provide suggestions to guide them—after giving sufficient time for them to explore and perform.

6. Play the recording, and have students perform the word chain with the track. Encourage students to speak the words as they clap the pattern.

7. Repeat by asking students to create additional word chains.

  Riff—Take a Solo: Create found-sound stations with unpitched percussion instruments in bins for students to explore and connect to their word chain. Invite individual students to share their choices and perform for the class.

Grade 1

First grade music is all about expression.

First grade learning focuses on students experiencing, sharing, making, and responding. Musical experiences should include a variety of activities that encourage creativity, allowing students to individually express themselves as they are introduced to formal musical concepts.

First grade musical experiences should include a variety of activities allowing students to explore the elements of classroom music while building skills and knowledge. Assessment at this level should be formative and include both individual and group engagement that focuses on skill development and demonstration—with teacher guidance.

Fundamentally, first grade music lessons include singing, playing, moving, listening, and reading—within the context of structured learning experiences that foster musical expression. In terms of jazz, first grade is the perfect setting to use this music as a prompt for students to imitate, create, and explore simple vocal, instrumental, and movement improvisation.

At the first grade level, the jazz-based teaching strategies presented in this book will engage students to respond, create, and perform, in the following ways.

LEARNING OUTCOMES

Respond

- Demonstrate steady beat (macrobeat and/or microbeat).
- Employ non-locomotor and/or locomotor movement.
- Express ideas verbally.
- Express personal decisions with rationale.
- Identify message, themes, and/or lyrical content.
- Imitate musical sounds and concepts.
- Move to reflect style of music.
- Use instruments or singing voice to express ideas.

Create

- Arrange patterns and/or movements.
- Create personal interpretations.
- Explore new ways to play instruments and/or use the voice.
- Explore new ways to use manipulatives in conjunction with music.
- Offer ideas for non-locomotor and/or locomotor movement.

Perform

- Perform chants, play-party games, stories, and/or poems with music.
- Perform individually.
- Perform original non-locomotor and/or locomotor movement.
- Perform rhythmic patterns.
- Perform simple body percussion.
- Perform simple dance and/or choreographed movement.
- Perform steady beat and melodic rhythm.
- Play classroom percussion instruments.
- Sing simple songs, melodic patterns, and/or melodies.
- Use manipulative/prop to depict a musical idea.

1.1. Taking Turns with Rhythm: Instrument Play

Learning Outcomes

Respond:

- Demonstrate steady beat (macrobeat and/or microbeat).
- Identify message, themes, and/or lyrical content.
- Imitate musical sounds and concepts.

Create:

- Create personal interpretations.

Perform:

- Perform simple body percussion.
- Perform steady beat and melodic rhythm.
- Play classroom percussion instruments.

Learning Targets

✓Listen ✓Move ✓Play

Music Selections

- "Taking a Chance on Love" Jane Monheit (*Taking a Chance on Love*, Sony Classical, 2004)
- "Taking a Chance on Love" Nancy Wilson (*Turned to Blue*, MCG Jazz, 2006)
- "Taking a Chance on Love" Ella Fitzgerald (*Sweet and Hot*, Verve Reissues, 1955)

Setup/Materials

- Space for movement; rhythm sticks, egg shakers

Teaching Strategy

1. Play the recording of "Taking a Chance on Love" by Jane Monheit, and encourage students to patsch the **steady beat** (macrobeat and microbeat—alternating between the two on the teacher's cue).

2. Demonstrate the **melodic rhythm** and have students speak and clap the words, "Taking a Chance on Love."

3. *Listen closely to hear the "Taking a Chance on Love" pattern each time it occurs in the music. Let's keep the steady beat until we hear it, and then clap and speak the pattern.*

> ## Cue
>
> Play the recording, and use a non-verbal cue (e.g., animated facial expression or other body language) to prepare students to perform the melodic rhythm pattern each time.

4. Divide students into two groups and distribute rhythm instruments:
   Group 1: **Rhythm Sticks**
   Group 2: **Egg Shakers**

5. Lead Group 1 to play the half-note macrobeat and Group 2 to play the quarter-note microbeat until they hear the melodic rhythm ("Taking a Chance on Love"), and play that pattern when it occurs.

6. *Now we will take turns to perform with instruments. Group 1 will go first, followed by Group 2. Then we will trade instruments and perform our patterns again. Watch to know when to play.*

> ## Cue
>
> To guide students in switching instruments, assign them to pairs or ask them to look around the room and find a person who has the opposite instrument they can trade with (using eye contact and/or pointing) in advance of the trade.

7. Play the recording, and lead students to play instruments.

   GROUP 1
(0:13 to 0:20)	Macrobeat
(0:21 to 0:24)	"Taking a Chance on Love" Melodic Rhythm

   GROUP 2
(0:25 to 0:31)	Microbeat
(0:22 to 0:34)	"Taking a Chance on Love" Melodic Rhythm

   GROUPS 1 AND 2
(0:35 to 0:46)	Switch Instruments
(0:47 to 0:54)	Macrobeat/Microbeat Together
(0:55 to 0:57)	"Taking a Chance on Love" Melodic Rhythm

 Riff: Play the recording of "Taking a Chance on Love" by Ella Fitzgerald and/or Nancy Wilson to provide opportunity for free instrument play (exploration) and "discovery" of a familiar song performed by a new artist.

1.2. Swinging Down the Railroad Tracks: Movement Imitation

Learning Outcomes

Respond:

- Demonstrate steady beat (macrobeat and/or microbeat).
- Express personal decisions with rationale.
- Move to reflect style of music.

Create:

- Create personal interpretations.

Perform:

- Perform individually.
- Perform rhythmic patterns.

Learning Targets

✓Connect ✓Describe ✓Imitate ✓Lead ✓Listen ✓Move

Music Selection

- "Choo, Choo, Ch' Boogie" Quincy Jones (*The ABC, Mercury Jazz Big Band Sessions*, Verve Reissues, 2011)

Setup/Materials

 Space for movement; pictures of a car, bicycle, airplane, and train on railroad tracks

 Set the Stage: Show pictures of a car, bicycle, airplane, and train. Ask students to raise their hand to identify the names of these forms of transportation.

Teaching Strategy

1. *Raise your hand if you have ever ridden... in a car* (show hands); *on a bicycle* (show hands); *on an airplane* (show hands); *on a train* (show hands).

2. *Today, we will hear a jazz song called "Choo, Choo, Ch' Boogie." This music is going to sound like one of our pictures. Raise your hand if you think "Choo, Choo, Ch' Boogie" is going to sound like a... car* (show hands); *bicycle* (show hands); *airplane* (show hands); *train* (show hands). *How did you decide?*

3. Play the recording of "Choo, Choo, Ch' Boogie," and ask students to chant with you as you speak the following pattern in a half-time feel:

   Train, Train, Choo Choo Train

   [Ta,   Ta,   Ta - di,   Ta]

   > ## Cue
   >
   > Invite students to copy a variety of non-locomotor movements (e.g., pointing arm gestures, rolling arms, clapping) to experience the follow-the-leader process and prepare for the locomotor movement.

4. Guide students to form a line (or circle moving in the same direction) and "walk down the railroad track" copying movements that match the "Train, Train, Choo Choo Train" pattern.

5. **Take a Solo:** *The conductor of the train is the driver.* Select individual student conductors to lead the train around the room and create movements for everyone to copy.

1.3. Ring the Bells: Instrument Sound/ No Sound

Learning Outcomes

Respond:

- Demonstrate steady beat (macrobeat and/or microbeat).
- Imitate musical sounds and concepts.
- Use instruments or singing voice to express ideas.

Create:

- Create personal interpretations.
- Explore new ways to play instruments and/or use the voice.

Perform:

- Perform rhythmic patterns.
- Play classroom percussion instruments.

Learning Targets

✓Describe ✓Improvise ✓Imitate ✓Listen ✓Move ✓Play

Music Selections

- "As Long as I'm Singing" Bobby Darin (*Wild, Cool & Swingin'*, Capitol Records, 1999)
- "Jersey Bounce" Ella Fitzgerald (*Work from Home with Ella Fitzgerald*, UMG Recordings, Inc., 2020)

Setup/Materials

- Jingle bells

Teaching Strategy

1. Play the recording of "As Long as I'm Singing" by Bobby Darin, and ask students to listen and sway to the macrobeat.

2. Distribute **jingle bells**, play the recording, and lead students to play the microbeat with their instruments.

3. *We will play a start and stop bell game. Watch to know when to play and when to be perfectly still.* Play the recording, and lead the game with a recurring pattern:

One Measure of Microbeat:	Ta-di,	Ta-di,	Ta-di,	Ta-di
One Measure of Rest:	Rest,	Rest,	Rest,	Rest

   > ## Cue
   > This game provides an opportunity for students to follow non-verbal directions. It may be difficult for bells to stop "jingling" during the freeze moments. Ask students to cup their free hand over the jingle bell to dampen the ringing.

4. *Now we will play the game again and this time our playing and stopping patterns will be longer. Watch to know when to play and when to stop and rest.* Play the recording, and lead the game with a recurring pattern:

Two Measures of Microbeat:	Ta-di,	Ta-di,	Ta-di,	Ta-di
Two Measures of Rest:	Rest,	Rest,	Rest,	Rest

5. *When you see this raised hand, you can play your bell any way you choose.* Play the recording, and guide students to **improvise** when your hand is raised and stop when your hand is lowered.

6. *Let's put this all together!* Lead students to perform the microbeat/rest recurring pattern until the interlude (0:40), improvise during the interlude (0:40 to 0:57), and perform the microbeat/rest pattern to the end.

   Riff: Invite students to perform a recurring macrobeat (Ta) measure/measure-of-rest pattern with the recording of Ella Fitzgerald's "Jersey Bounce" (improvising during the scat solo beginning at 0:12 and returning to play patterns 2:11 to the end).

7. *How did you make your bells stop ringing each time we rested?*

   > ## Cue
   > Asking students to reflect and evaluate personal actions/behaviors and ability to follow directions will help build this habit and support feelings of accomplishment and pride.

1.4. Jazzy Spider Charades: Movement Game

Learning Outcomes

Respond:

- Employ non-locomotor and/or locomotor movement.
- Express personal decisions with rationale.
- Move to reflect style of music.

Create:

- Create personal interpretations.
- Offer ideas for non-locomotor and/or locomotor movement.

Perform:

- Perform individually.
- Perform original non-locomotor and/or locomotor movement.
- Sing simple songs, melodic patterns, and/or melodies.

Learning Targets

✓Improvise ✓Lead ✓Listen ✓Move ✓Sing

Music Selection

- "Itsy Bitsy Spider" Jazz at Lincoln Center Orchestra, arr. Wynton Marsalis (*Jazz for Kids*, Blue Engine Records, 2019)

Setup/Materials

- Space for movement; (optional: movement cards/pictures)

Teaching Strategy

1. Lead students in singing the traditional "Itsy Bitsy Spider" song with accompanying hand motions.

2. *Today, we are going to listen to a jazzy version of this song and perform our "Itsy Bitsy Spider" hand motions with the track. Be sure to listen for the familiar tune.* Play the recording, and lead students to sing and perform the traditional hand motions.

3. *Let's move like jazzy spiders! How do you think a jazzy spider moves?* Play the recording, and have students explore ways to move like jazzy spiders.

4. *When we create something on the spot, it is called* **improvisation***. We will be improvising several ways to move as we listen to this jazzy spider music.* Play the recording, and call out prompts for students to follow (e.g., tie shoes, brush teeth, play guitar).

5. **Take a Solo:** Invite individual students to share movement ideas for everyone to imitate.

6. Divide students into groups to prepare for the Charades game. Encourage groups to work together to create a secret group movement (e.g., swim, jump rope, throw and catch a ball).

> ## Cue
> Remind students to keep their group movement idea a secret to facilitate the Charades game.

7. Play the recording, and invite groups in turn to demonstrate their movements for everyone to guess.

> ## Cue
> The recording is used to create an environment/set the scene for movement improvisation. It is not necessary for students to match movements to reflect the beat or style of the music.

Riff: Create a set of teacher-made cards with pictures showing a variety of movements (e.g., tie shoes, brush teeth, jump rope) to prompt movements performed by the groups.

1.5. Hittin' the Town: Movement Exploration

Learning Outcomes

Respond:

- Employ non-locomotor and/or locomotor movement.
- Express ideas verbally.
- Identify message, themes, and/or lyrical content.

Create:

- Create personal interpretations.
- Offer ideas for non-locomotor and/or locomotor movement.

Perform:

- Perform original non-locomotor and/or locomotor movement.

Learning Targets

✓Connect ✓Describe ✓Improvise ✓Listen ✓Move

Music Selections

- "Top Hat, White Tie, and Tails" Louis Armstrong (*American Jazz—Irving Berlin Songs*, U-5, 2013)
- "Top Hat, White Tie, and Tails" Fred Astaire (*Mr. Top Hat*, Verve Reissues, 1957)
- "It's a Good, Good Night" Peggy Lee (*Ultra Lounge: Wild, Cool & Swingin' 3!*, Capitol Records, 2009)

Setup/Materials

 Space for movement; picture of a person wearing a top hat and tuxedo

 Set the Stage: Show pictures and lead students to associate attire with a location or action: pajamas (bed), swimsuit (beach), workout clothes (gym), etc.

Teaching Strategy

1. Play the recording of "Top Hat, White Tie, and Tails," by Louis Armstrong. *The singer in this music is a famous jazz artist named Louis Armstrong. When we listen to the words of the song, we hear that he is getting dressed up for something. Raise your hand if you can tell me what he is putting on for his outing.*

2. Display a picture of someone dressed in a top hat and tuxedo. *Raise your hand if you have ever gotten dressed up in a fancy outfit.*

3. *Where could you be going if you were dressed up like this?* List answers on the board. Ask students to vote on their favorite.

> ## Cue
> Asking students questions about personal experiences and preferences allows for reflection and real-world connections.

4. *Now we are going to pretend that we are getting ready for a fancy outing. Let's put a pretend top hat on our head to get ready.* Play the track, and have students act out the lyrics in the song.

5. *Let's listen to Fred Astaire's version of the song and perform a fancy party walk. Remember that you have a pretend top hat on your head, and let the music tell you how to move.*

> ## Cue
> This is an opportunity for free movement exploration and personal expression.

 Riff—Take a Solo: Play Peggy Lee's "It's a Good, Good Night," and invite students to perform a new fancy party walk.

6. *How did you perform your fancy party walk? What decisions did you make to create it?*

1.6. Painting with Scarves: Dance the Form

Learning Outcomes

Respond:

- Express personal decisions with rationale.
- Identify message, themes, and/or lyrical content.
- Move to reflect style of music.

Create:

- Create personal interpretations.
- Explore new ways to use manipulatives in conjunction with music.
- Offer ideas for non-locomotor and/or locomotor movement.

Perform:

- Perform individually.
- Perform simple dance and/or choreographed movement.
- Use manipulative/prop to depict a musical idea.

Learning Targets

✓Connect ✓Describe ✓Improvise ✓Listen ✓Move

Music Selection

- "What a Wonderful World" Louis Armstrong (*What a Wonderful World*, GRP, 1968)

Setup/Materials

- Space for movement; scarves

Teaching Strategy

1. *Today, we will listen to a song called "What a Wonderful World." In the song, the singer named Louis Armstrong paints a picture of his view of a wonderful world.*

2. Play the recording, and guide students to listen for colors. *What colors did you hear in the song?* (Green, Red, Blue, White)

3. *Let's act like musical "painters" with scarves.* Distribute scarves and have students stand.

4. Play the recording, and guide students to dip their scarf in a bucket of pretend paint and move it like a paintbrush to paint the images in the lyrics (e.g., trees, roses, sky, clouds, day, night, friends shaking hands, me and you).

    Riff: Ask students to pretend to paint the classroom with their scarves to make it an even more wonderful music world.

5. Teach students the following scarf motions to reflect the **AABA** form and perform with the recording.

   A Section: Move scarf up and down like a paintbrush while walking around the room (locomotor)

   B Section: Toss scarf in the air and catch it while standing in place (non-locomotor)

6. Play the recording, and allow students to create their own scarf movements on the B section.

    7. **Take a Solo:** Select students to take turns and individually perform their B section scarf movements, and then speak the name of another student to perform next.

    Riff: Have students create scarf movements for the A and B sections in small groups.

1.7. The Alphabet: Like Do, Re, Mi—Sing and Chant

Learning Outcomes

Respond:

- Imitate musical sounds and concepts.
- Express ideas verbally.

Create:

- Create personal interpretations.

Perform:

- Perform chants, play-party games, stories, and/or poems with music.
- Play classroom percussion instruments.
- Sing simple songs, melodic patterns, and/or melodies.

Learning Targets

✓Connect ✓Describe ✓Improvise ✓Listen ✓Move ✓Play ✓Sing

Music and Chant Selections

- "The Alphabet: Like Do, Re, Mi" Darla S. Hanley
- "The New ABC" Lambert, Hendricks & Ross (*The Hottest New Group in Jazz*, Columbia/Legacy, 1996)

Setup/Materials

- Space for movement; (optional: prepared xylophones or other barred instruments, mallets)

 Set the Stage: Invite students to play a game of "I Spy with My Little Eye" to find objects in the music room that begin with a specific letter of the alphabet (e.g., "B" for Bells, "D" for drums).

Teaching Strategy

1. Teach the following chant by rote:

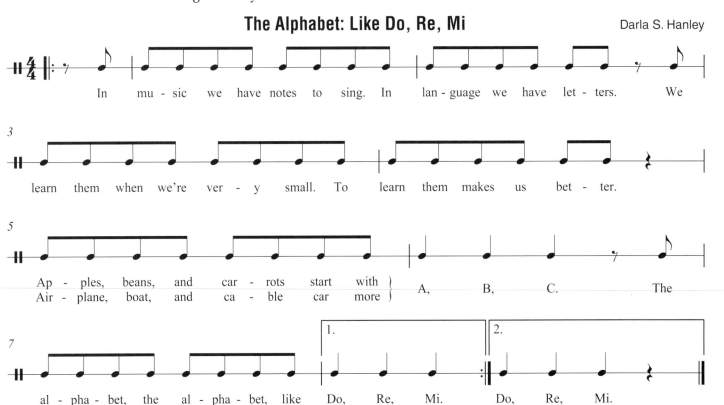

FIG. 1.7. The Alphabet: Like Do, Re, Mi Chant

> ## Cue
>
> Teach one stanza at first, building to add two, three, and then all four stanzas over time.

2. Ask students to sing the familiar "ABC Song" either a cappella or with an accompaniment.

3. *We will hear a recording of the "ABC Song" in a jazzy style performed by musicians named Lambert, Hendricks & Ross. Let's listen closely to hear them sing all of the letters. They will sing the alphabet two times in a row. Be ready to tell me what happens the second time they sing the "ABC Song."*

4. Play the first 1:18 of the recording and encourage students to "think" the song in their head as they listen.

5. Lead a discussion about the **tempo** of the song getting faster the second time.

6. *We are going to sing the "ABC Song" with the recording. Be ready to get faster the second time.* Play the recording, and lead students to sing.

7. *Now let's add our chant to happen after we sing the song. Follow my lead to know when to begin.*

> ## Cue
>
> **Important Note:** You need to anticipate the entrance of the chant and begin over the vocal falloff at the end of the "ABC Song" and stay within the rhythmic framework to be able to perform the full chant within the instrumental interlude.

8. Play the recording of "The New ABC," and ask students to sing along, chant during the instrumental interlude, and sing to the end.

9. *What happened after our chant?* (The music got even faster and then slow again like the beginning.)

> ## Cue
>
> The track transitions to up-tempo swing at 2:04 after the instrumental interlude followed by a ("tell me what you think of me") tag. It then returns to the slow/opening tempo of the alphabet song, but ends on "L, M, N, O, P," so you may want to point that out or ask to see if students noticed.

 Riff: Prepare **xylophones** or other barred instruments to only have "C, D, E" (i.e., Do, Re, Mi) available. Invite students to perform the chant without a track and select one student to play the "Do, Re, Mi" pattern when it occurs each time while the other students either whisper the solfege or "think" the solfege syllables while performing corresponding hand signs.

 Riff: Guide students to play Do, Re, Mi on prepared xylophones or other barred instruments, and improvise freely to explore new ways to play these three notes.

1.8. We ♥ Jazz: Dance

Learning Outcomes

Respond:

- Employ non-locomotor and/or locomotor movement.
- Move to reflect style of music.

Create:

- Create personal interpretations.

Perform:

- Perform original non-locomotor and/or locomotor movement.
- Perform simple dance and/or choreographed movement.

Learning Targets

✓Describe ✓Imitate ✓Listen ✓Move

Music Selections

- "L-O-V-E" Michael Bublé (*Call Me Irresponsible [Deluxe]*, Atlantic Records, 2007)
- "L-O-V-E" Nat King Cole (*L-O-V-E*, Capitol Records, 1992)
- "I Can't Give You Anything but Love" Sarah Vaughan (*Sassy Swings the Tivoli*, Verve Reissues, 1963)

Setup/Materials

- Space for movement

 Set the Stage: Take photos of members of the school community (e.g., teachers, paraprofessionals, principal, school nurse, janitor, cafeteria staff, bus drivers) performing the LOVE spelling movements to post in the school lobby or other main area with a "We ALL ♥ Jazz" banner.

Teaching Strategy

1. *Today, we will listen to two jazz songs about love, "L-O-V-E" and "I Can't Give You Anything but Love." Raise a hand if you can tell me something you love. Think of some of your favorite songs. What do you love most about music?*

> ### Cue
> Asking students questions about personal experiences and preferences allows for reflection and real-world connections.

2. Invite students to stand and imitate movements (spelling LOVE).

> ## Cue
> Speak the letter as you form its shape to anchor movements.

L: Right arm straight up, left arm straight out at shoulder height creating an "L" shape.

O: Both arms over head creating an "O" shape.

V: Both arms up and out creating a "V" shape.

E: The "L" move with the right arm arched over the head, an added left leg out, the left toe pointed on the floor.

3. Play the recording of "L-O-V-E" by Michael Bublé, and invite students to listen for the letters and move to spell the word "LOVE" each time. (Hold the shape of each letter until the next letter occurs.)

> ## Cue
> Repeat the first 0:40 of this track to practice LOVE spelling moves.

4. *Now that we know our LOVE spelling moves, we will add more to our dance. Watch closely to know how to move.*

5. Play the recording, and lead students to perform the LOVE spelling moves, and to copy swaying, heart pumps, and freestyle movements.

> ## Cue
> Sing along with the recording as you demonstrate movements to informally engage students in singing this song. The initial focus is for movement/movement exploration; however, another option is to teach "L-O-V-E" by rote.

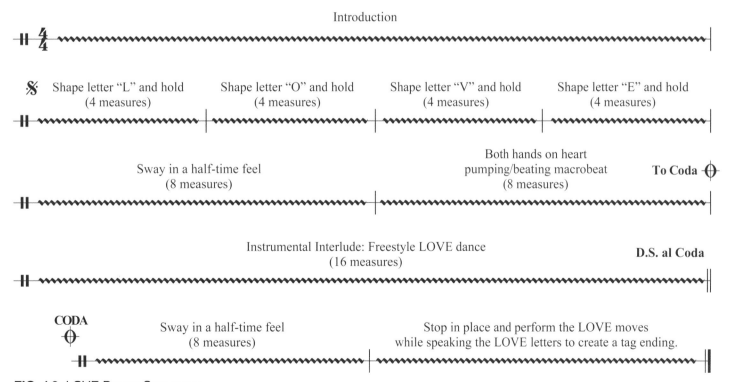

FIG. 1.8. LOVE Dance Sequence

 Riff: Perform the dance with the Nat King Cole recording of "L-O-V-E."

 Riff: Play the recording of "I Can't Give You Anything But Love" by Sarah Vaughan, and ask students to perform the LOVE spelling moves. Invite students to create four-beat movements to perform in alternation with the "LOVE spelling moves" to make a movement accompaniment for the track.

1.9. Tea Cups for Two: Play Rhythms

Learning Outcomes

Respond:

- Demonstrate steady beat (macrobeat and/or microbeat).
- Use instruments or singing voice to express ideas.

Create:

- Arrange patterns and/or movements.
- Create personal interpretations.
- Explore new ways to use manipulatives in conjunction with music.

Perform:

- Perform rhythmic patterns.
- Perform simple body percussion.
- Play classroom percussion instruments.

Learning Targets

✓Arrange ✓Listen ✓Play ✓Read

Music Selection

- "Tea for Two Cha Cha" Tommy Dorsey Orchestra featuring Warren Covington (*Tea for Two Cha Cha*, Remastered, Take Five Music, 2018)

Setup/Materials

- Maracas, cowbell, sets of tea cup cards

 Set the Stage: Create a "Tea Cup Rhythms" bulletin board near the door to your classroom to reinforce iconic notation with four large and eight small pictures of tea cups. Arrange them in patterns, and allow students to practice clapping and/or speaking the rhythms using rhythm syllables as they enter and exit the classroom.

Teaching Strategy

1. Arrange four tea cup cards (showing large tea cups) on the board. Play the recording of "Tea for Two Cha Cha," and have students patsch the macrobeat as you point to the cards.

2. Arrange eight tea cup cards (showing small tea cups) on the board. Play the recording, and have students patsch the microbeat as you point to the cards.

3. Arrange a four-beat pattern using both large and small tea cup cards. Play the recording, and have students clap as you point to the tea cups to create an **ostinato**.

> ## Cue
>
> This is an opportunity to introduce or reinforce **repeat signs** and the concept of ostinati.

4. **Take a Solo:** Arrange a pattern on the board, and ask individual students to perform it with the recording.

5. *Now we're going to work with partners and create a four-beat tea cup pattern to perform for the class. Each pair will get a set of tea cup cards, a **cowbell**, and **maracas**. You will need to decide who plays which instrument and use both large and small tea cups in your patterns.*

6. Play the recording, and invite all students to play their patterns at the same time to practice.

7. **Take a Solo:** Invite pairs to arrange their tea cup cards on the board and perform with the recording.

Riff—Take a Solo: Have students switch instruments and create an eight-beat ostinato by combining two original four-beat rhythmic patterns with their partner to perform with the recording.

1.10. Blue Skies and Happy Dances: Dance

Learning Outcomes

Respond:

- Employ non-locomotor and/or locomotor movement.
- Move to reflect style of music.

Create:

- Create personal interpretations.
- Offer ideas for non-locomotor and/or locomotor movement.

Perform:

- Perform individually.
- Perform original non-locomotor and/or locomotor movement.
- Perform simple dance and/or choreographed movement.

Learning Targets

✓Connect ✓Describe ✓Improvise ✓Imitate ✓Lead ✓Listen ✓Move

Music Selection

- "Blue Skies" Rosemary Clooney (*From Bing to Billie*, Concord Records, 2004)

Setup/Materials

- Space for movement

 Set the Stage: *What color is the sky on a sunny summer day?* (Blue) *What is something you like to do on a sunny summer day that makes you happy?*

Teaching Strategy

1. *Let's listen to a jazz song called, "Blue Skies" and do a happy dance to show the style of this music.*

> ## Cue
>
> A "happy dance" is moving in a way that makes you happy—there are no "wrong" responses. Demonstrate a variety of shoulder, head, arm, and knee "happy" movements to prompt students.

2. Ask students to imitate the three movements needed for the "Sunshine and Bluebirds Dance" (i.e., swaying hands, flapping arms, open-and-close hands). Play the recording, and guide students to practice these movements.

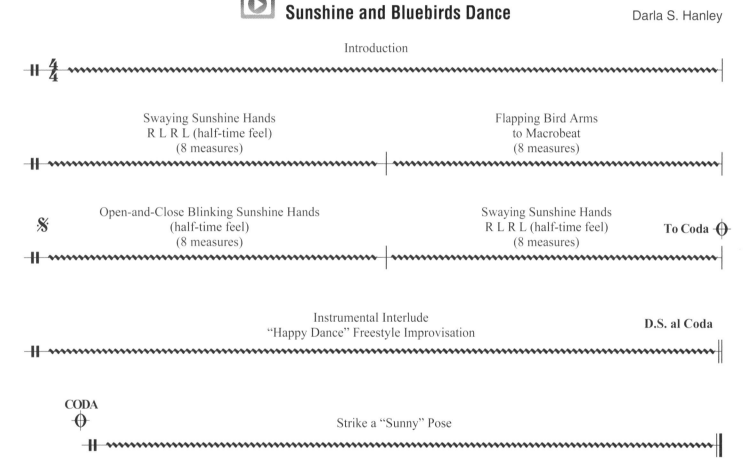

FIG. 1.10. Sunshine and Bluebirds Dance Sequence

3. *Now we will perform a dance with sunshine hands and happy dance moves. When the singer stops singing, we will hear musical instruments playing the lead part. Listen closely for those instruments, and do a "happy dance" until the singer returns. Watch to know what to do!*

> ## Cue
>
> The improvised solos (the "happy dance section") go from 0:49 to 2:47 of this track. This dance works with the full track or with an excerpt.

 Riff—Take a Solo: Select individual students to create a happy dance move for everyone to copy during the instrumental solos.

Grade 2

Second grade music is all about making musical choices.

Second grade learning focuses on students expressing personal preferences and making decisions. Musical experiences here should include a variety of activities that provide students with opportunities to make musical choices individually and with others. At this level students are able to listen and describe music, collaborate in ensembles, work with partners, perform movements and formalized dances, create patterns, read simple music notation; and use personal preferences in music to make informed choices.

Fundamentally, second grade music lessons include singing, playing, moving, listening, and reading—within the context of structured learning experiences that foster music making and musical choice. Assessment should be formative and summative and include opportunities for individual and group demonstrations. In terms of jazz, second grade is the perfect setting for students to continue to do things such as imitate musical sounds and concepts, offer original ideas, feel the groove of a tune, trade fours, create scat syllables, identify form, and improvise individually and within a group, for example.

At the second grade level, the jazz-based teaching strategies presented in this book will engage students to respond, create, and perform, in the following ways.

LEARNING OUTCOMES

Respond

- Demonstrate steady beat (macrobeat and/or microbeat).
- Employ non-locomotor and/or locomotor movement.
- Express ideas verbally.
- Imitate musical sounds and concepts.
- Listen and describe music.
- Make musical decisions.
- Move to reflect style of music.
- Use instruments or singing voice to express ideas.

Create

- Create personal interpretations.
- Create rhythmic patterns on instruments and/or with body percussion.
- Create scat/nonsense syllables.
- Offer ideas for non-locomotor and/or locomotor movement.

Perform

- Perform chants, play-party games, stories, and/or poems with music.
- Perform dance and/or choreographed movement.
- Perform individually.
- Perform original non-locomotor and/or locomotor movement.
- Perform rhythmic patterns.
- Perform simple body percussion.
- Perform with a partner.
- Play classroom percussion instruments.
- Use manipulative/prop to depict a musical idea.

2.1. This Is Kathy's Waltz: Body Percussion

Learning Outcomes

Respond:

- Demonstrate steady beat (macrobeat and/or microbeat).
- Employ non-locomotor and/or locomotor movement.
- Listen and describe music.

Create:

- Create personal interpretations.
- Offer ideas for non-locomotor and/or locomotor movement.

Perform:

- Perform rhythmic patterns.
- Perform simple body percussion.

Learning Targets

✓Describe ✓Imitate ✓Listen ✓Move

Music Selections

- "Kathy's Waltz" The Dave Brubeck Quartet (*Time Out*, Columbia/Legacy, 1959)
- "Kathy's Waltz" Quartet San Francisco (*QSF Plays Brubeck*, Violinjazz Recordings, 2009)

Setup/Materials

- Space for movement

 Set the Stage: Create an "Instruments of Jazz" bulletin board in the music room or school lobby to showcase the musicians and instruments studied in music class.

Teaching Strategy

1. *Today, we will listen to jazz music called "Kathy's Waltz," performed by pianist Dave Brubeck and his quartet then by a group called Quartet San Francisco.*

> ## Cue
>
> Use the first 1:06 excerpt of the Brubeck track and first 1:07 excerpt of the Quartet San Francisco track for this movement exploration.

2. *Listen closely and be ready to describe the music you hear.* Play the recording of "Kathy's Waltz" (Brubeck), and lead a discussion.

3. Play the recording again, and invite students to clap and speak the following pattern in a half-time feel:

   This is   Ka-thy's Waltz
   Ta, Ta, Ta-di,   Ta

4. Observe students, and once they are able to perform the pattern consistently, lead them to perform it using a variety of non-locomotor **body percussion** (e.g., patsch, tap toes, tap shoulders).

5. *Now we will hear "Kathy's Waltz" performed by Quartet San Francisco. Listen closely to find the same song, and be ready to tell me what **instruments** you hear this time.* Lead a discussion about the instruments that make up a **string quartet**.

6. Play the Quartet San Francisco recording, and ask students to create body percussion movements to perform as they speak the "This is Ka-thy's Waltz" pattern.

 Riff—Take a Solo: Guide students to stand in a circle and turn to face a partner. Ask partners to create four-beat body percussion combinations as they speak the "This is Ka-thy's Waltz" pattern. Play the Brubeck recording and select pairs to go to the center and perform movements for everyone to copy.

 Riff: Ask students to create four-beat movements (locomotor) instead of non-locomotor body percussion.

2.2. Too Cool Conversations: Trade Solos

Learning Outcomes

Respond:

- Demonstrate steady beat (macrobeat and/or microbeat).
- Imitate musical sounds and concepts.
- Use instruments or singing voice to express ideas.

Create:

- Create personal interpretations.

Perform:

- Perform with a partner.
- Play classroom percussion instruments.

Learning Targets

✓Describe ✓Improvise ✓Listen ✓Move ✓Play

Music Selection

- "Cool Struttin'" Sonny Clark (*Cool Struttin' [Remastered/Rudy Van Gelder Edition]*, Blue Note Records, 1958)

Setup/Materials

- Variety of rhythm instruments

 Set the Stage: Create a monthly "Meet the Artists" bulletin board to showcase artists studied per grade level.

Teaching Strategy

1. Play the recording of "Cool Struttin'," and ask students to move their shoulders to show the **steady beat** or **pulse** of the music.

> ## Cue
>
> Asking students to listen and demonstrate steady beat without further instruction or modeling will illustrate their understanding of beat concept.

2. Distribute a variety of rhythm instruments, and ask students to form partners. Select one student per pair to become the first person to create a four-beat rhythmic pattern for their partner to copy. Perform patterns with the recording. Switch roles and repeat.

3. Next, ask students to have a musical conversation with their partner using rhythm instruments—creating a four-beat rhythmic pattern that is a question followed by their partner performing a four-beat rhythmic pattern answer. *In jazz this is called **trading fours**.*

4. Play the recording, and invite students to perform musical conversations with the track.

> ## Cue
>
> At this level, the intent is to have students create patterns in turn, not necessarily create patterns that relate Q&A style or include specific elements beyond four beats. Additionally, the track is meant to anchor the rhythms and exchange while allowing students to become familiar with the sound of jazz.

 Riff: Invite students to switch instruments and/or switch partners to perform new musical conversations.

5. *What words would you use to describe the experience of trading fours, if you were having a conversation with a friend?*

2.3. Rondo Interpretations: Play the Form

Learning Outcomes

Respond:

- Express ideas verbally.
- Imitate musical sounds and concepts.
- Use instruments or singing voice to express ideas.

Create:

- Create personal interpretations.
- Create rhythmic patterns on instruments and/or with body percussion.

Perform:

- Perform rhythmic patterns.
- Play classroom percussion instruments.

Learning Targets

✓Connect ✓Describe ✓Imitate ✓Listen ✓Play

Music Selections

- "The Syncopated Clock" Quincy Jones (*The ABC, Mercury Jazz Big Band Sessions*, Verve Reissues, 2011)
- "The Syncopated Clock" Percy Faith and His Orchestra (*The Essential Percy Faith – The Instrumental Recordings*, Legacy Recordings, 2018)

Setup/Materials

- Rhythm instruments by category (e.g., woods, metals, drums)

Teaching Strategy

1. *Today, you will hear two recordings of music called, "The Syncopated Clock." The first one is by Percy Faith and His Orchestra. This music is divided into parts or sections, which when put together, create something we call "**rondo** form" (i.e., ABACA).*

2. Ask students to listen to the recording and raise their hand each time the A section occurs.

> ### Cue
> Wait to observe students and their ability to identify the A section each time before you raise a hand. At first, mention the B section when it occurs (and the same with the C section) to familiarize students with the sounds and the form of this music.

3. Play the recording again, and ask students to stay seated and raise a hand during the A section each time, stand up when they hear the B section, and stay seated and shake jazz hands when they hear the C section.

4. Ask students to speak and clap the following rhythmic patterns and label as Pattern A, Pattern B, and Pattern C.

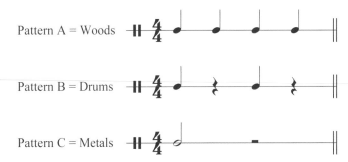

FIG. 2.3. Rondo Rhythmic Patterns

5. Distribute tick-tocks, rhythm sticks, drumsticks, woodblocks, and/or claves to a group of students. Lead a discussion to name the instruments and categorize them as "**woods**."

6. Ask students with instruments in the "woods" category to play Pattern A each time the A section occurs.

> ### Cue
> Ask students without instruments to tap the macrobeat or pretend they have instruments and "play" along.

7. Distribute drums to a second group of students and lead a discussion to name the instruments (e.g., hand drum, bongo, conga), and categorize them as "**drums**."

8. Play the recording, and have the "woods" perform Pattern A during the A section and "drums" perform Pattern B during the B section.

9. Distribute bells and tambourines to a third group of students, and lead a discussion to label these instruments as "**metals**." Ask this group to perform Pattern C during the C section when it occurs.

10. *Now we are going to listen to a jazz interpretation of "The Syncopated Clock" by a producer named Quincy Jones, and play our rondo percussion patterns with the track.* Play the recording, and cue the "ABACA" rondo sections as they occur.

> ### Cue
> There is a brief interlude ahead of the C section in the Quincy Jones track where you will need to guide students to listen closely and let the music tell them when to begin playing the metals. Asking them to "groove" during the interlude is a jazzy way to fill the extra space.

 Riff: Have students trade instruments, and repeat to vary and expand their instrument play experience.

11. *How many sections were in our rondo form today?*

> ### Cue
> Guide students to connect the A, B, and C sections with instruments as a clue, if needed.

 Riff: Invite students to create original rhythmic patterns to perform during the B and/or C section.

2.4. Jazz Cats Scat: Scat Patterns

Learning Outcomes

Respond:

- Express ideas verbally.
- Imitate musical sounds and concepts.
- Listen and describe music.

Create:

- Create personal interpretations.
- Create scat/nonsense syllables.

Perform:

- Perform chants, play-party games, stories, and/or poems with music.
- Perform rhythmic patterns.

Learning Targets

✓Arrange ✓Connect ✓Imitate ✓Listen ✓Move

Music and Chant Selections

- "Hey Diddle Dwee Dat" Allison P. Kipp
- "Splanky" Count Basie (*The Atomic Mr. Basie*, Parlophone UK, 1958)

Setup/Materials

- Seated in a circle

Teaching Strategy

1. Teach "Hey Diddle Dwee Dat" by rote (whole-part-whole).

Hey Diddle Dwee Dat

Allison P. Kipp

FIG. 2.4a. Hey Diddle Dwee Dat Chant

2. *Today, we will create nonsense syllables to form a B section to go along with the chant. What is the name for nonsense syllables in jazz music?* (**Scat**)

3. Invite students to imitate the following scat pattern:

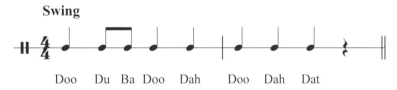

FIG. 2.4b. Scat Pattern

4. Play the recording of "Splanky" by Count Basie, and ask students to speak the scat pattern.

   Riff: Ask students to speak the scat pattern with the recording, and clap or perform body percussion to show the rhythm.

5. *Now we will put this together to create an ABA composition!* Invite students to perform the chant (A section), scat pattern (B section), and chant (A section) with the recording.

> ## Cue
> Begin the chant after the introduction at 0:11.

6. Ask students to select scat syllables from the pattern, and reassign them to the rhythms to create a new scat syllable arrangement for the B section (e.g., "Dat, doo-doo, dah, dat, doo, doo, doo"). Play the recording, and perform the new **ABA** composition.

2.5. Rhythm a Go-Go: Instrument Play

Learning Outcomes

Respond:

- Demonstrate steady beat (macrobeat and/or microbeat).
- Imitate musical sounds and concepts.
- Use instruments or singing voice to express ideas.

Create:

- Create personal interpretations.
- Create rhythmic patterns on instruments and/or with body percussion.

Perform:

- Perform rhythmic patterns.
- Play classroom percussion instruments.

Learning Targets

✓Improvise ✓Listen ✓Move ✓Play ✓Read

Music Selection

- "Pick Yourself Up" Dianne Reeves (*Good Night, Good Luck*, Concord Records, 2005)

Setup/Materials

- Cowbell, conga, maracas, güiro

 Set the Stage: Display a poster or slide showing images of cowbell, conga, maracas, and güiro. Invite students to come to the front to point to the instrument to either "find" it in the picture or "be the teacher" and point to it for all to see.

Teaching Strategy

1. Teach the following parts by asking students to read and clap rhythms.

> ### Cue
>
> Inserting syllables (Ta, Ta-di) beneath the rhythms will assist students in reading music notation as they develop these skills.

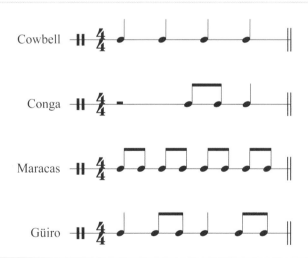

FIG. 2.5. Rhythmic Patterns for Instrument Groups

2. Divide students into the four instrument groups. Distribute rhythm instruments, and transfer parts from body percussion to the cowbell, conga, maracas, and güiro.

Cue

This learning experience works with just about any rhythm instrument. If available, substitute agogo bells for cowbell, timbales for conga, egg shakers for maracas, and kokorico for güiro to add variety.

3. Play the recording of "Pick Yourself Up," and ask students to follow your lead, like musicians follow a **conductor**. *Watch to know when it's your group's turn to play.*

Cue

Begin playing instruments when vocals enter at 0:15. There is an instrumental interlude from 1:17 to 1:47. Asking students to watch and play upon a non-verbal signal provides an opportunity for students to build self-control.

4. Ask students to listen for the part of the song where the singer stops singing and instruments continue. *This is called an **instrumental interlude**. During the instrumental interlude, you can make musical decisions to play your instruments any way you choose to reflect the jazz music. Remember to explore new ways of playing, and only play in your most musical manner.*

Cue

Providing opportunities for free musical exploration fosters artistic freedom, personal expression, and independence.

 Riff: Invite two instrument groups to play their rhythmic patterns (at the same time) with the recording, and ask all students/instruments to improvise during the interlude. Repeat with the remaining two instrument groups.

 Riff—Take a Solo: Ask students to play together to create a "rhythm section" accompaniment using the patterns, and select individual students to improvise as a soloist in the ensemble.

2.6. Jazz Takes a Walk: Improvised Movements

Learning Outcomes

Respond:

- Demonstrate steady beat (macrobeat and/or microbeat).
- Employ non-locomotor and/or locomotor movement.
- Move to reflect style of music.

Create:

- Create personal interpretations.
- Offer ideas for non-locomotor and/or locomotor movement.

Perform:

- Perform individually.
- Perform original non-locomotor and/or locomotor movement.
- Perform with a partner.

Learning Targets

✓Describe ✓Improvise ✓Imitate ✓Listen ✓Move

Music Selections

- "Thunderwalk" George Benson and Harold Lomax Ousley (*History*, U-5, 2014)
- "On Broadway" Nicki Parrott (*From New York to Paris*, ARBORS, 2019)
- "My Little Suede Shoes" Charlie Parker (*20th Century Masters: The Millennium Collection – The Best of Charlie Parker*, Verve Reissues, 2004)

Setup/Materials

- Space for movement

Teaching Strategy

1. *Today, we will take a jazz walk as we listen to music called "Thunderwalk" performed by a* **guitarist** *named George Benson. What do you think a jazz walk is?* Lead responses to original ways of walking to reflect the jazz music, moving and grooving, etc.

2. Play the recording, and guide students to march in place, move shoulders, and/or bob head, etc. to reflect the style.

> **Cue**
>
> Beginning with non-locomotor movements will anchor this learning experience and prepare students for locomotor engagement.

3. *Now we will take the feeling of the movements we performed in place and put them into our jazz walk. Listen closely to the music and create a new way of walking that shows what you hear. Remember, you can walk tall or small, backwards or forward. Be sure to watch out for each other as you go, and if you like something you see someone else doing, give it a try!*

> **Cue**
>
> Encourage free expression and original ideas by asking students to create movements without providing specific examples. Observe students and offer suggestions or prompts, as needed.

4. Play the recording, and lead students in "jazz walking" around the room.

> ## Cue
> Use a jazzy voice and offer the following phrases to encourage students as they move: "Let's take a walk," "a jazzy walk," "oh, yeah, let's walk," "look at us walk."

5. *What does it mean to trade?* (To exchange, share) *In jazz music, musicians trade solos on instruments or with their voices. Now, we are going to trade jazz walks.*

6. Ask students to form a circle, and select one student to create a jazz walk movement—"walking" into the center to show the movement and then "walking" up to another student—trading places (i.e., selecting a new student to "walk" and then trade).

> ## Cue
> Set the length of time spent "walking" by individual students or provide direction such as, "Cool jazz walking, do your best, time to trade so who is next." Repeat with as many "jazz walkers" as time permits.

7. *Now I'm going to change the music for our jazz walks. Listen closely for the **acoustic bass** instrument playing the melody.*

8. Play "On Broadway" by Nicki Parrott, and continue the jazz walk movement game.

   Riff: Play the recording of "My Little Suede Shoes" by Charlie Parker, and repeat the jazz walk movement game.

> ## Cue
> The jazz walk movement game provides an opportunity to expose students to a variety of jazz music, as long as the tempo is suitable to "walking."

   Riff: Ask students to form partners, stand facing each other, and create four-beat "jazz walking" movements to trade.

9. *How did you change the way you walked to fit the music and make it jazzy?*

2.7. Judge's Choice: Rhythmic Pattern Contest

Learning Outcomes

Respond:

- Express ideas verbally.
- Listen and describe music.
- Make musical decisions.

Create:

- Create personal interpretations.
- Create rhythmic patterns on instruments and/or with body percussion.

Perform:

- Perform rhythmic patterns.
- Perform simple body percussion.
- Play classroom percussion instruments.

Learning Targets

✓Compose ✓Describe ✓Listen ✓Move ✓Play

Music Selection

- "A-Tisket A-Tasket" Ella Fitzgerald (*100 Songs for a Centennial*, Verve Reissues, 2017)

Setup/Materials

- Space for movement; tambourines

 Set the Stage: Create a "Meet the Band" bulletin board to showcase famous jazz artists.

Teaching Strategy

1. *Today, we will listen to music by Ella Fitzgerald and create rhythmic patterns in groups.*

2. Play the recording of "A-Tisket A-Tasket," and have students describe the **tempo** and **mood**. Invite students to move around the room to reflect the style of the piece.

3. Play the recording again, and perform four-beat rhythmic patterns using body percussion for students to echo (e.g., clap, stomp, patsch, snap).

4. Divide students into two groups and distribute **tambourines**.

5. *We will be working in our groups to create four-beat rhythmic patterns to play on our instruments with the recording.*

6. Guide students to create a four-beat body percussion pattern, and then transfer it to their tambourine.

> ## Cue
> Asking groups of students to create together provides an opportunity for leadership and consensus building.

7. *Now that you have created your rhythmic patterns, let's play a "Judge's Choice Game." We will have a judge's panel of students who will make musical decisions to select a winner based on the group's ability to create and perform four-beat rhythmic patterns. If you are on the judge's panel, you need to listen closely and look for things like steady beat and everyone working together to create a group sound as you evaluate.*

> ## Cue
> Providing opportunities for healthy competition encourages students to establish positive behaviors and good sportsmanship.

8. Select four students (two per group) to form the judge's panel and begin the game. Invite Group 1 to perform their rhythms with the recording followed by Group 2.

    Riff: Invite classroom teachers to form the judge's panel.

> ## Cue
> - When students are not performing, they will be audience members. Remind them to be good listeners and show their best manners as others perform.
> - Guide judges to compare observations/deliberate to select the winner.

9. *How did it feel to perform in the "Judge's Choice Game"? How did you demonstrate audience behavior and good sportsmanship?*

> ## Cue
> Asking students to reflect on personal feelings and behaviors establishes a healthy habit of self-evaluation.

2.8. Rollin' and Steppin' to the Groove: Movement with Form

Learning Outcomes

Respond:

- Listen and describe music.
- Make musical decisions.
- Move to reflect style of music.

Create:

- Create personal interpretations.
- Offer ideas for non-locomotor and/or locomotor movement.

Perform:

- Perform original non-locomotor and/or locomotor movement.

Learning Targets

✓Connect ✓Listen ✓Move

Music Selection

- "Step Lightly (Junior's Arrival)" Clifford Brown (*Clifford Brown and Max Roach at Basin Street [Expanded Edition]*, Verve Reissues, 1990)

Setup/Materials

- Space for movement; large foam dice

Teaching Strategy

1. Play the recording of Clifford Brown's "Step Lightly (Junior's Arrival)," and have students walk around the room to the macrobeat and "feel" the groove. Encourage students to move using different levels (e.g., low, middle, high).

2. Assign movements to represent the A and B sections (e.g., flap chicken-wing arms = A section; skip = B section).

> ## Cue
>
> The form of the music is: **AABA**, followed by an improvisation section, and ending with another A section. The improvisation section begins at 1:10 and the A section returns at 3:08.

3. Play the recording, and invite students to move throughout the space (locomotor), changing movements when they hear the section change.

4. Write the following movements and numbers on the board:

   1. Cool Walk
   2. Butterfly Swim
   3. Shoulder Bounce
   4. Up-Down Shimmy
   5. Flick the Wrist
   6. Bobble Head Nod

5. Play the recording, and call movements from the list for students to perform around the room. Guide students to make musical decisions, encouraging them to move to show the sound of the music.

6. *Now, we will play a game and let the dice tell us which movement to perform.* Play the recording, roll the die, and call out movements. Continue rolling the die and calling movements.

   Riff: Invite students to create a new list of movements to assign to numbers 1 to 6, roll the die, and perform with the recording.

   Riff: Assign various die numbers "move of your choice," and roll frequently during the improvisation section.

2.9. Pie Pan Partners: Dance

Learning Outcomes

Respond:

- Demonstrate steady beat (macrobeat and/or microbeat).
- Employ non-locomotor and/or locomotor movement.
- Express ideas verbally.

Create:

- Create personal interpretations.
- Offer ideas for non-locomotor and/or locomotor movement.

Perform:

- Perform dance and/or choreographed movement.
- Perform with a partner.
- Use manipulative/prop to depict a musical idea.

Learning Targets

✓Describe ✓Imitate ✓Lead ✓Listen ✓Move

Music Selection

- "Shoo Fly Pie and Apple Pan Dowdy" June Christy with Stan Kenton and His Orchestra (*Collection 1945–1955*, ACROBAT, 2019)

Setup/Materials

- Space for movement; disposable (foil) pie pans

 Set the Stage: Collaborate with the art teacher to create an art project for students to decorate personal foil pie pans (to post, use to perform, or take home).

Teaching Strategy

1. *Let's listen to a song called "Shoo Fly Pie and Apple Pan Dowdy" performed by June Christy and the Stan Kenton Orchestra. The Stan Kenton Orchestra was a **jazz band**. Based on that information, what do you think you will hear?* (Guide responses to singer, jazz big band, song about dessert)

> ## Cue
>
> Asking students to predict sounds based on song titles or other clues provides an opportunity for critical and creative thinking and the ability to apply prior knowledge.

 Riff: Play the recording, and invite students to sing the title of the song when they hear it each time it occurs.

2. Distribute pie pans (one per student), and teach the following "Pie Pan Routine":

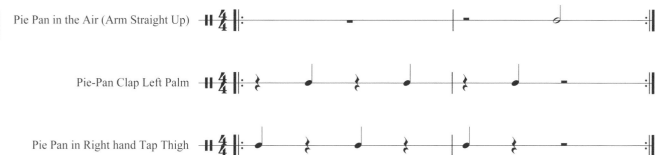

FIG. 2.9. Pie Pan Routine

3. Invite students to perform the "Pie Pan Routine" with the recording.

> ## Cue
>
> Encourage students to move their shoulders and groove during the introduction and begin the routine at 0:15.

4. Ask students to form partners and perform the "Pie Pan Routine" in pairs by replacing the pie-pan clap on their own palm with a pie-pan clap (pan-to-pan) with their partner.

 Riff—Take a Solo: Ask students for suggestions of other ways to tap rhythms using their pie pan (individually or with a partner). Select one student to create a new way to "play the pan" for everyone to copy.

2.10. We're Getting Fruity: Tambourine Improvisations

Learning Outcomes

Respond:

- Employ non-locomotor and/or locomotor movement.
- Make musical decisions.
- Use instruments or singing voice to express ideas.

Create:

- Create personal interpretations.

Perform:

- Perform chants, play-party games, stories, and/or poems with music.
- Perform individually.
- Play classroom percussion instruments.

Learning Targets

✓Improvise ✓Listen ✓Play

Music and Chant Selections

- "Tangerine" Bucky Pizzarelli (*Green Guitar Blues/Café Pierre Trio*, Audiophile, 2001)
- "We're Getting Fruity" Darla S. Hanley

Setup/Materials

- Tambourine(s)

Teaching Strategy

1. Play the recording of "Tangerine" by Bucky Pizzarelli, and tell students the name of the song and the artist.

2. *Now, we're going to play* **tambourines** *and* **improvise** *with this song as part of a musical game. Remember, "improvise" means we make musical decisions and create on the spot. This game is called "We're Getting Fruity."* Speak the chant and inform students that they will play the tambourine to improvise when their name is called.

We're Getting Fruity

Darla S. Hanley

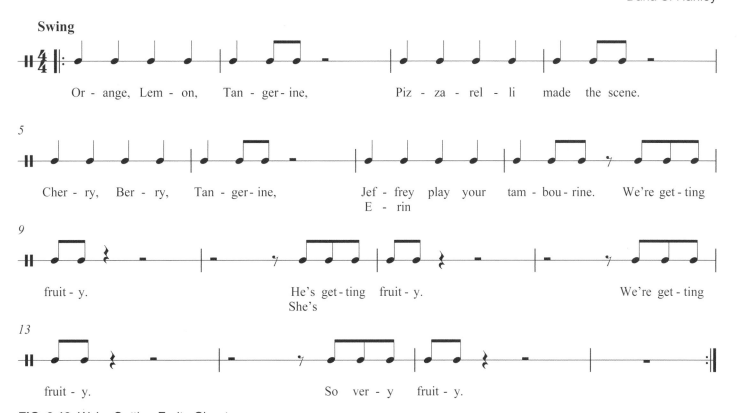

FIG. 2.10. We're Getting Fruity Chant

3. **Take a Solo:** Select a student to begin and insert that student's name in the chant (i.e., INSERT NAME, *play your tambourine*). Play the recording, begin the game, and repeat with several student soloists as time permits.

> # Cue
> Be jazzy and syncopated in the speech delivery of this chant to really get fruity!

Riff: Distribute several tambourines, and ask all students with instruments to simultaneously improvise using the variation, "players, play your tambourines."

Grade 3

Third grade music is all about fostering musical independence.

Third grade learning focuses on individual abilities and skill development. Musical experiences here should include a variety of activities that foster collaboration among students while simultaneously encouraging independent music making. At this level, students are able to collaborate in ensembles, work with partners, perform unstructured and formalized dances and/or movements, create arrangements and accompaniments, read traditional music notation, and use personal preferences in music to make decisions individually and within a group.

Fundamentally, third grade music lessons include singing, playing, moving, listening, reading, and creating—within the context of structured learning experiences that promote personal ownership of skills/knowledge. Assessment should be formative and summative and include opportunities for individual and group demonstrations. In terms of jazz, students at this level are able to do things such as describe musical elements, themes, and patterns; improvise individually and within a group; feel the groove of a tune; and imitate and offer original ideas to create using instruments and/or body percussion; for example.

At the third grade level, the jazz-based teaching strategies presented in this book will engage students to respond, create, and perform, in the following ways.

LEARNING OUTCOMES

Respond

- Demonstrate steady beat (macrobeat and/or microbeat).
- Employ non-locomotor and/or locomotor movement.
- Express ideas verbally.
- Express personal decisions with rationale.
- Follow aural cues.
- Listen and describe music.
- Move to reflect style of music.
- Use instruments or singing voice to express ideas.

Create

- Arrange patterns and/or movements.
- Create personal interpretations.
- Create rhythmic patterns on instruments and/or with body percussion.
- Offer ideas for non-locomotor and/or locomotor movement.

Perform

- Perform body percussion.
- Perform dance and/or choreographed movement.
- Perform in two or more parts.
- Perform individually.
- Perform original ideas to create an accompaniment.
- Perform original non-locomotor and/or locomotor movement.
- Perform rhythmic patterns.
- Perform with a partner.
- Play classroom percussion instruments.
- Play or sing while reading rhythmic and/or melodic notation.

3.1. Everybody's Playin': Steady Beat and Melodic Rhythm

Learning Outcomes

Respond:

- Demonstrate steady beat (macrobeat and/or microbeat).
- Follow aural cues.
- Listen and describe music.

Create:

- Create personal interpretations.
- Offer ideas for non-locomotor and/or locomotor movement.

Perform:

- Perform body percussion.
- Perform rhythmic patterns.
- Play classroom percussion instruments.

Learning Targets

✓Listen ✓Move ✓Play

Music Selection

- "Everybody's Jumpin'" The Dave Brubeck Quartet (*Time Out*, Columbia/Legacy, 1959)

Setup/Materials

- Chairs in a circle (seats facing out); single rhythm instrument per chair

Teaching Strategy

> ## Cue
>
> This game is designed to work best using the first 1:24 of the track. Position instruments under the chairs to begin so students can sit while focusing on **melodic rhythm** and the guidelines of the game.

1. *Today, we will play instruments in a game that is similar to Musical Chairs. Raise your hand if you are familiar with that game.*

2. *Listen closely for a repeating melodic rhythm pattern in the music.* Demonstrate the melodic rhythm pattern of the phrase "Everybody's Jumpin', jump, jump," and have students speak and clap it.

3. Play the recording of "Everybody's Jumpin'," and invite students to listen for the melodic rhythm pattern of "Every-body's Jum-pin', jump, jump" and speak/clap it when it occurs.

4. Invite students to get the instrument from under their chair and play the melodic rhythm pattern each time it occurs within the recording.

5. *Now, we will stand and place our instruments on the seat of our chair. We will play a rotating rhythm instrument game where we will walk in a circle around the chairs, stopping when we hear the melodic rhythm pattern and playing it on the instrument on the chair in front of us. When that pattern ends, place your instrument back on the chair, and resume walking.*

6. Guide students to explore different ways to walk to show the sounds of the music and listen closely to let the music tell them what to do. Play the recording, and begin the game.

> ## Cue
>
> The "Everybody's Jumpin'" melodic pattern happens three times within the first 1:24 of the track. Guide students to listen closely to hear the melodic rhythm pattern each time and carefully place instruments back on chairs as the game continues.

 Riff: Invite students to turn and walk in the opposite direction to play the game following a vocal cue from the teacher.

3.2. Dixieland Duos: Play-Party Game

Learning Outcomes

Respond:

- Demonstrate steady beat (macrobeat and/or microbeat).
- Employ non-locomotor and/or locomotor movement.
- Express personal decisions with rationale.

Create:

- Create personal interpretations.
- Create rhythmic patterns on instruments and/or with body percussion.

Perform:

- Perform body percussion.
- Perform individually.
- Perform with a partner.

Learning Targets

✓Compose ✓Describe ✓Imitate ✓Lead ✓Listen ✓Move

Music Selection

- "Up a Lazy River" Wycliffe Gordon (*Hello Pops! A Tribute to Louis Armstrong*, Blues Back, 2011)

Setup/Materials

- Space for movement; (optional: photos of play-party movements)

 Set the Stage: Take photos of students performing play-party game movements to post in the classroom or on the internal school website.

Teaching Strategy

1. *We are going to hear music in a Dixieland jazz style called "Up a Lazy River," performed by* **trombonist** *Wycliffe Gordon with his* **Dixieland band***.*

2. *Let's listen to this music and move our shoulders to* **groove** *and show its style and tempo.*

3. Invite students to form partners, and teach the following play-party game (using words from the song lyrics, "La-zy Ri-ver, Old Mill Run" to anchor the movements):

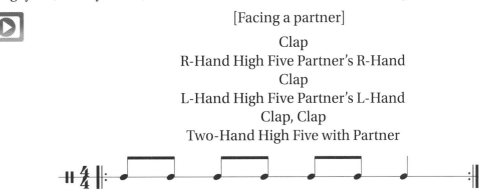

[Facing a partner]

Clap
R-Hand High Five Partner's R-Hand
Clap
L-Hand High Five Partner's L-Hand
Clap, Clap
Two-Hand High Five with Partner

FIG. 3.2. Lazy River Rhythmic Anchor

4. *Let's perform our movements with the recording of "Up a Lazy River."*

> ## Cues
> - Guide students to listen closely, and let the music lead them to know when to begin at 0:08, following the brief introduction.
> - There is an up-tempo scat break (1:24 to 1:42) where students can perform their play-party movements in the new fast tempo, or dance/groove in a freestyle manner until the music lets them know when to return to their play-party pattern.

5. Invite students to compose their own play-party game movement sequence with their partner (using the lyrics "La-zy Riv-er, Old Mill Run" to anchor movements).

6. Divide the class into two groups. Ask Group 2 to sit and watch as Group 1 performs their play-party game with the recording. Repeat with Group 2 performing.

> ## Cue
> This is an opportunity to evaluate students and observe how they evaluate each other.

7. *How did you work together to create an original play-party game with your partner? Which original play-party game stood out to you, and what made it special?*

8. **Take a Solo:** Select students to teach their play-party game to the class for everyone to perform.

   Riff: Select three play-party games and create an **ABACA** "Play-Party Rondo"—assigning one play-party game to represent each of the A, B, and C sections.

   Riff: Take and use photos of students performing movement ideas as prompts for new combinations. Put photos in a box, and have students draw one picture at a time to create movements.

3.3. Monk Moving Statues: Move and Freeze Dance

Learning Outcomes

Respond:

- Follow aural cues.
- Listen and describe music.
- Move to reflect style of music.

Create:

- Create personal interpretations.
- Offer ideas for non-locomotor and/or locomotor movement.

Perform:

- Perform original non-locomotor and/or locomotor movement.

Learning Targets

✓Connect ✓Improvise ✓Listen ✓Move

Music Selection

- "In Walked Bud" Thelonious Monk (*Genius of Modern Music Volume One*, CM Blue Note [A9]), 2013)

Setup/Materials

- Space for movement

Teaching Strategy

1. Play the recording of "In Walked Bud," and have students raise their hand when they hear the A section and shout out when they hear the B section.

> ## Cue
>
> Use the first 0:45 of the track to focus on **AABA** form, and repeat as needed to reinforce the students' ability to listen and label sections.

2. Assign students to Group A and Group B, ask them to find a spot in the room where they can stretch their arms out without touching anything, and strike a pose.

3. *We are going to become statues and moving statues as we listen to "In Walked Bud" by a musician named Thelonious Monk.*

4. *Group A will move around the room during the A section while the B Group holds their pose like a statue. When the B section happens, Group A will strike and hold a pose while Group B moves around the room. Listen and move to show the sound of the music when it's your turn and hold your pose as still as you can when you are a statue.*

5. Play the recording, and invite students to listen and move.

> ## Cue
>
> Call out sections to guide students until they demonstrate understanding of form.

 Riff: Assign each group a level such as high, medium, or low to encourage movement in new pathways.

 Riff: Ask students to switch groups and repeat with the recording.

3.4. USA States in Improv: Arranging Word Chains

Learning Outcomes

Respond:

- Employ non-locomotor and/or locomotor movement.
- Express ideas verbally.
- Listen and describe music.

Create:

- Arrange patterns and/or movements.
- Create rhythmic patterns on instruments and/or with body percussion.

Perform:

- Perform body percussion.
- Perform original ideas to create an accompaniment.
- Perform with a partner.

Learning Targets

✓Arrange ✓Compose ✓Connect ✓Describe ✓Listen ✓Move ✓Play

Music Selection

- "(Get Your Kicks on) Route 66" The Nat King Cole Trio (*Ultimate Nat King Cole*, Capitol Catalog Market [C92], 2019)

Setup/Materials

 Space for movement; USA map, pins, variety rhythm instruments; (optional: USA state name cards)

 Set the Stage: Post a map of the United States in the room as a reference. Invite students to put a "pin" in every state they include in their improvisations at the end of the class.

Teaching Strategy

1. Play the recording of "(Get Your Kicks on) Route 66" by the Nat King Cole Trio, and ask students to tell you what they hear. Guide responses to: instruments, state names, and city names; a song about traveling across the United States/traveling down the highway named Route 66.

2. *Let's make a list of the cities and states we heard in the song. Which ones are cities and which ones are states?*

> ### Cue
>
> Cities: Chicago, L.A. (Los Angeles), St. Louis, Joplin, Oklahoma City, Amarillo, Gallup, Flagstaff, Winona, Kingman, Barstow, San Bernardino
>
> States: Missouri, New Mexico, Arizona, and California

3. *Today, we will use the names of states within the United States to create a jazz **improvisation** to **accompany** the recording.*

4. Project a map of the USA, and identify the states mentioned in the song.

5. Randomly point to individual states, and ask students to echo you as you speak state names. Go from speaking states randomly to forming a chain of state names (e.g., Utah, Texas, Kansas, Maine; California, Idaho) and asking students to echo the chain.

6. Once you create a string like, "Utah, Texas, Kansas, Maine" or "California, Idaho" ask students to speak the combination with the recording.

7. Invite students to form partners. *With your partner, you will **compose** a four-beat USA state pattern. First, select the names of up to four USA states you want to include in your pattern. The melodic rhythm of the words will tell you how many beats they fill. Start with two state names, and add more until your pattern is four beats long. Once you choose the state names, work with your partner to **arrange** them in a specific order, and practice that sequence. Next, create movements or body percussion to show the rhythm of the state names, and practice your combinations.*

> ## Cue
> Demonstrate a "patsch-clap, patsch-clap, stomp, stomp, stomp" movement pattern to go with the melodic rhythm of the "California, Idaho" state improv as an example.

8. Ask students to form two lines facing each other, standing across from their partner. Play the recording, and invite all students to practice their state patterns with the track.

9. *Now, we will create a state accompaniment for the track by having partners perform patterns two times in a row, in turn, moving down the line. We will start at one end of the line and continue until all pairs have performed. Listen closely as the patterns move down the line to hear the accompaniment, and be ready when it's your turn!*

> ## Cue
> Invite students to begin performing after the introduction at 0:20, and prepare the first pair to be ready to start again when the last partners in the line perform.

 Riff: If space allows, divide the class into two two-line formations (or more) to perform their patterns down the line and provide greater opportunity to repeat/perform.

 Riff: Replace body percussion/movements with rhythm instruments.

 Riff: Create USA state name cards, and put them in a bag for students to draw to create a chain of patterns using the melodic rhythm of the state with a corresponding movement or rhythm instrument.

3.5. Rhumba Rhythms: Instrument Play

Learning Outcomes

Respond:

- Express ideas verbally.
- Listen and describe music.
- Use instruments or singing voice to express ideas.

Create:

- Create rhythmic patterns on instruments and/or with body percussion.

Perform:

- Perform in two or more parts.
- Play classroom percussion instruments.
- Play or sing while reading rhythmic and/or melodic notation.

Learning Targets

✓Connect ✓Describe ✓Listen ✓Play ✓Read

Music Selections

- "Peanut Vendor" Anita O'Day (*Sings the Winners*, Verve Reissues, 1958)
- "The Peanut Vendor" Stan Kenton and His Orchestra (*The Best of Stan Kenton*, Blue Note Records, 1995)

Setup/Materials

- Maracas, claves, güiros

 Set the Stage: Create a "Now Featuring: Latin Jazz" bulletin board that highlights Latin music, notable works, and instruments.

Teaching Strategy

1. *Close your eyes, and imagine that you are at a sporting event. Think about the sounds you hear and the smells of the delicious food. You may see someone walking around to sell you food at your seat. These people are called vendors. What types of food do they sell?* Guide responses to: cotton candy, soda, pretzels, peanuts, cracker jacks, hot dogs, etc.

2. *We will hear a recording about a vendor selling something. Listen closely and be ready to tell me what they sell.* (Peanuts)

3. *This song is called "Peanut Vendor" and is performed by Anita O'Day. Later we will play instruments with this music.*

4. Display the rhythm ensemble notation, and guide students to read and clap the patterns.

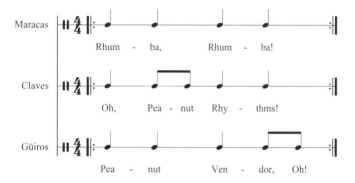

FIG. 3.5. Rhumba Rhythms

5. Divide students into three groups and distribute instruments (Group 1: **Maracas**; Group 2: **Claves**; Group 3: **Güiros**). Play the recording, and have students perform their assigned group pattern on their instruments.

> ## Cue
> Substitute instruments to vary the learning experience and reinforce other shakers, drums, and scrapers.

6. Ask groups to work together to create a new four-beat pattern (using Ta and Ta-di rhythms) to perform on their instrument with corresponding words about foods sold by vendors.

7. *Now we will listen to a recording of "The Peanut Vendor" by Stan Kenton and His Orchestra. Listen closely to this new version, and be ready to compare it to the one by Anita O'Day.* Lead a discussion.

8. Invite groups to perform their original patterns with the Stan Kenton recording for everyone to observe. Repeat until all groups have performed.

> ## Cues
> - Students will need to perform their patterns in a half-time feel due to the upbeat tempo of the Kenton recording.
> - This is an opportunity to evaluate students and observe how they evaluate each other.

Riff: Create an **ABACA** "Rhumba Rondo" with the original patterns as the A section and ideas from individual groups to use for the B and C sections.

3.6. Howdy Hay Dance: Dance

Learning Outcomes

Respond:

- Employ non-locomotor and/or locomotor movement.
- Move to reflect style of music.

Create:

- Create personal interpretations.
- Offer ideas for non-locomotor and/or locomotor movement.

Perform:

- Perform dance and/or choreographed movement.
- Perform original non-locomotor and/or locomotor movement.

Learning Targets

✓Describe ✓Imitate ✓Listen ✓Move

Music Selection

- "Hay Burner" Count Basie (*Straight Ahead*, Verve Reissues, 1998)

Setup/Materials

- Space for movement

Teaching Strategy

1. Play the recording of "Hay Burner" by Count Basie, and lead students to walk around the room to reflect the sound of the music. Ask them to greet the other students and explore ways to speak the word "hay" to them as they move.

Cues

- Demonstrate a variety of ways of saying "hay" with movement (e.g., "hay, snap, hay, snap, hay, snap, hay"; sustained "H-a-a-a-y"; staccato "Hay, hay, hay"; high/low voice). This is an opportunity to informally introduce the music before teaching a choreographed dance. The vocal exploration with the word "hay" adds a playful element and encourages students to use eye contact and offer friendly greetings.
- Ask students to define "hay" and "hey" for clarification between spellings and meanings (i.e., grass and greeting).

2. Ask students to stand in four rows with everyone facing the board to create straight lines, and teach the following dance steps:

Board

X   X   X   X

X   X   X   X

X   X   X   X

X   X   X   X

FIG. 3.6. Formation for Howdy Hay Dance

> **Cue**
>
> Adjust the number of lines based on the number of students and space available to dance.

Position = Hands on Hips or with Thumbs in (Pretend) Belt Loops

Tap R Heel on the Floor
Cross R in Front of L and Tap R Toe on the Floor
Tap R Heel on the Floor (same as first time)
Step R Down with Feet Together

Tap L Heel on the Floor
Cross L in Front of R and Tap L Toe on the Floor
Tap L Heel on the Floor (same as first time)
Step L Down with Feet Together

(Repeat from the top)

Grapevine R (Step R, L Behind, Step R, Step Down with Feet Together)
Grapevine L (Step L, R Behind, Step L, Step Down with Feet Together)

Step Touch R, L, R, L with Lasso Arm Spinning an Imaginary Rope (turning to the L to face a new direction on the second R L step touch—a quarter turn)

3. Play the recording, and lead students to perform the dance with the track.

> **Cue**
>
> Allow lots of practice time at a slow tempo, increasing to the speed of the music before adding the track. Begin dance steps at 0:17, following the introduction.

Riff: Ask students to create new arm movements to perform in place of the Lasso Arms during the Step Touches.

3.7. Drummers Meet Shakers: Instrument Groups

Learning Outcomes

Respond:

- Demonstrate steady beat (macrobeat and/or microbeat).
- Listen and describe music.
- Use instruments or singing voice to express ideas.

Create:

- Arrange patterns and/or movements.
- Create personal interpretations.
- Create rhythmic patterns on instruments and/or with body percussion.

Perform:

- Perform rhythmic patterns.
- Perform with a partner.
- Play classroom percussion instruments.

Learning Targets

✓Arrange ✓Compose ✓Describe ✓Listen ✓Play ✓Read

Music Selections

- "Begin the Beguine" Artie Shaw (*The Essential Artie Shaw*, Bluebird/Legacy, 2005)
- "Waltz for Debby" Allen Toussaint (*American Tunes*, Nonesuch, 2016)

Setup/Materials

- Drums, maracas, egg shakers

Teaching Strategy

1. Distribute drums to half of the class and shakers to the other half. *You are going to hear a recording of jazz music called "Begin the Beguine" featuring Artie Shaw as a* **clarinet soloist** *with a* **jazz band**. *Listen closely to the music and play your best accompaniment with your* **drum** *or* **shaker**. *Remember to hold the instrument properly and explore a variety of accompaniment rhythms.* Play the recording of "Begin the Beguine," and invite students to freestyle an accompaniment.

> ### Cue
> Providing time for students to play instruments freely (without guidelines) gives them ownership of their music making and builds independence.

2. Display the following rhythmic patterns for students to read and play on their instruments:

FIG. 3.7. Rhythmic Patterns

3. Review the term **ostinato** and invite students to arrange the three rhythmic patterns to create an ostinato sequence to perform with the recording.

> ## Cue
>
> Begin playing at 0:07 following the introduction.

4. *What is the same about our three patterns?* (All include Ta and Ta-di, Ta-di happens on beat 2 of each pattern.)

5. Ask students with drums to work together and students with shakers to work together to compose a four-beat pattern using Ta, Ta-di, and Rests.

> ## Cue
>
> Write the word "drums" on the board, and notate the pattern composed by the drum group so students can see the combination of Ta, Ta-di, and Rests, and have a pattern available as a reference while playing. Repeat with shakers.

6. *Now you will play your new group pattern by instruments in turn. Drums will go first then shakers come right in, so we create a two-group ostinato. Watch to know when to start playing. Be sure to listen closely to the other musicians when it's not your turn to play.*

> ## Cue
>
> This is an opportunity to discuss the role of a **conductor** in music and talk about how musicians listen to each other when they play and sometimes need to rest and wait quietly before adding their contribution to the music making.

7. Ask students to form pairs (one drum/one shaker), and invite them to **arrange** patterns to create a new ostinato to perform with the track.

   Riff: Invite students to trade instruments and repeat.

   Riff: Repeat with "Waltz for Debby" by Allen Toussaint. *Close your eyes, and listen to the recording. Raise your hand when you hear a Ta, Ta-di, Ta, Ta pattern played on drums and shakers. Join in to play this pattern on your instrument when you are ready to play.*

> ## Cue
>
> Encouraging students to listen with eyes closed, and to raise a hand to show what they hear, removes peer pressure and/or the opportunity for students to follow each other. Once most begin playing the patterns on instruments, ask everyone to open their eyes and continue playing.

3.8. Entrances and Exits: Improvised Movements

Learning Outcomes

Respond:

- Employ non-locomotor and/or locomotor movement.
- Express personal decisions with rationale.
- Move to reflect style of music.

Create:

- Create personal interpretations.
- Offer ideas for non-locomotor and/or locomotor movement.

Perform:

- Perform individually.
- Perform original non-locomotor and/or locomotor movement.
- Play classroom percussion instruments.

Learning Targets

✓Describe ✓Improvise ✓Listen ✓Move ✓Play

Music Selections

- "Walkin' in Music" Gary Burton (*Next Generation*, Concord Records, 2005)
- "Groovin' Hard" Groove for Thought (*Groovin' Hard*, Groove for Thought, 2018)
- "Groovin' Hard" (Alternate Take, Live) Buddy Rich (*Jazz Cats: Drum*, Remixed and Remastered, U-5, 2014)

Setup/Materials

- Space for movement; claves; (optional: music stickers)

 Set the Stage: Decorate the door of the music room with images of artists "entering" a stage (on the outside/hallway side of the door) and images of artists "exiting" a stage (to post on the inside door leading back to the hallway).

Teaching Strategy

1. Ask students to form a circle, and select one student to begin the game. *Our game is called "Entrances and Exits," and we are going to play it with a song called "Walkin' in Music" by Gary Burton.*

2. **Take a Solo:** *When you are selected, you will walk into the center of the circle, create a movement that matches the sound of the music, and then "cut though" the other side of the circle. Make a "V" shape with your hands (palms/wrists touching) to inform the other students where you will exit/ cut through. Then you will go around the outside of the circle walking and moving to show the jazz music until you choose the next person by tapping them on the shoulder. You can only walk around the circle one time, so be sure to choose someone before you get back to your original spot. Once you choose someone, you will take their space in the circle, and they will go to the center, create a move, cut through, walk, and choose.*

3. Play the recording of "Walkin' in Music" and begin the game.

> ## Cue
> Have students put a sticker on the shoulder of the student they choose when they tap. This will help everyone keep track of who has had a turn, and will give students a music sticker for the day!

Riff—Take a Solo: Distribute a pair of **claves** to one student. Remind students of the name of this instrument and how to hold/play it. Invite that student to go to the center of the circle to improvise over four measures of the music, use the claves to create the "V" shape to indicate the cut through, walk and play around the outside of the circle until they select the next student, and repeat.

> ## Cue
> Lead the students in the circle to count the **measures** (1, 2, 3, 4; 2, 2, 3, 4; 3, 2, 3 4; 4, 2, 3, 4) to deepen their engagement and guide the soloist to keep track of timing.

Riff: Repeat the game with the recording of "Groovin' Hard" by Groove for Thought and "Groovin' Hard" by Buddy Rich. *Which music did you like best for this game? How did you make your decision?*

> ## Cue
> Providing students with opportunities to share personal preference with a rationale helps them develop a habit of confident decision-making and expression.

3.9. Ready, Play, Switch: Instruments on Cue

Learning Outcomes

Respond:

- Demonstrate steady beat (macrobeat and/or microbeat).
- Follow aural cues.
- Use instruments or singing voice to express ideas.

Create:

- Create personal interpretations.
- Create rhythmic patterns on instruments and/or with body percussion.

Perform:

- Perform individually.
- Perform rhythmic patterns.
- Play classroom percussion instruments.

Learning Targets

✓Connect ✓Describe ✓Imitate ✓Listen ✓Move ✓Play

Music Selection

- "Wrap Your Troubles in Dreams" Sarah Vaughan (*The Divine One*, Remaster: Parlophone UK, 2007)

Setup/Materials

- Lummi sticks/wooden dowels

Teaching Strategy

1. *Let's listen to a recording of a jazz **vocalist** named Sarah Vaughan singing "Wrap Your Troubles in Dreams." Be ready to tell me how this song makes you feel.*

2. *While we listen, let's cross our arms over our body like we are wrapping ourselves in a great big hug, and **groove** by moving our shoulders to show the music.*

3. Play the recording, and groove/move. Lead a discussion to allow students to share their emotional response to the music.

> ### Cue
> Depending on student responses, this may be an opportunity to discuss how music changes our mood, how favorite music makes us happy, how music inspires us to dance, etc.

4. Distribute **Lummi sticks** or wooden dowels (two per student). Remind students of the name of the instrument and how to hold and play it.

> ### Cue
> **Lummi sticks** or wooden dowels are "fatter," which provides a larger playing surface, but rhythm sticks or claves could also work here.

5. Ask students to imitate a variety of rhythmic patterns with the sticks that include Ta and Rests.

> ### Cue
> Limiting options to quarter notes and quarter rests will allow space for students to focus on and explore new ways to play the sticks (e.g., tapping on the floor, crossing sticks to tap together with an "X").

6. Teach Parts 1 and 2, and ask students to play them on their instrument.

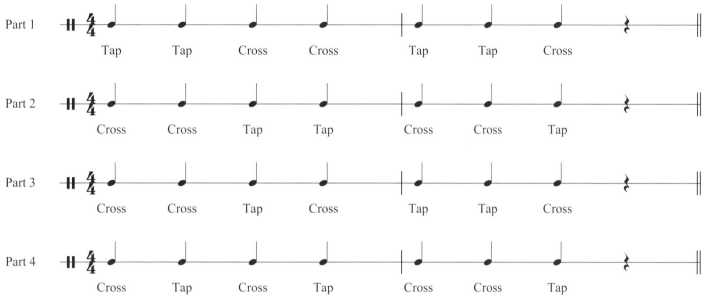

FIG. 3.9. Cross and Tap Rhythms

7. Play the recording, and ask students to play Parts 1 and 2 in sequence (repeating like an ostinato).

> ## Cues
> - It may be necessary to highlight the repeated "cross" transition from Part 1 to Part 2 to guide students.
> - Once students become comfortable with the parts, introduce the idea of switching.

8. *Now we are going to change it up. Instead of playing Parts 1 and 2 in order, you will play Part 1 over and over until you hear "switch." When you hear the word "switch," begin playing Part 2. When you hear "switch" again, go back to playing Part 1. Listen closely, here we go!*

9. Play the recording, and lead students to play (and switch) parts.

> ## Cue
> You will need to anticipate speaking the word "switch" near the end of the previous part to prepare students to make the change and continue with the steady pulse of the recording.

10. Ask students to explore new combinations of tapping and crossing sticks (using Ta and Rest) to perform with the track. Play the recording, and provide time for practice.

 11. **Take a Solo:** Select individual students to demonstrate their rhythm combination with the track. Ask individuals to teach their part for everyone to play.

12. Introduce Parts 3 and 4, and repeat the instrument play.

13. *Which parts do you like best, 1 and 2, or 3 and 4? Why? Do you find them all the same to play? How did you make your decision?*

> ## Cue
> Asking students to share preferences and reflect on the complexity of a task establishes habits of personal expression and healthy self-evaluation.

 Riff: Ask students to form partners, and play Parts 1 and 2, or Parts 3 and 4, tapping the floor for the "taps" and tapping their partner's sticks for the "cross" each time.

3.10. Finding Partners: Discover Movements

Learning Outcomes

Respond:

- Demonstrate steady beat (macrobeat and/or microbeat).
- Employ non-locomotor and/or locomotor movement.
- Listen and describe music.

Create:

- Create personal interpretations.
- Offer ideas for non-locomotor and/or locomotor movement.

Perform:

- Perform original non-locomotor and/or locomotor movement.
- Perform with a partner.

Learning Targets

✓Connect ✓Listen ✓Move

Music Selection

- "A Wink and a Smile" Harry Connick, Jr. (*Sleepless in Seattle: Original Motion Picture Soundtrack*, Epic Soundtrax, 1993)

Setup/Materials

 Space for movement; movement cards (in pairs)

Teaching Strategy

1. *Let's listen to "A Wink and a Smile" by Harry Connick, Jr., and move in place to show the **steady beat**.* Play the recording, and call out movements such as tap head, hop, clap, flap chicken wing arms, and wiggle for students to perform.

2. *This music is in **AABA** form.* Play the recording, and ask students to stroll around the room during the A section (0:06 to 0:39; 0:59 to 1:16) and stand in place and "lift the sky" (palms up pulsing the macrobeat) to the B section (0:40 to 0:58).

FIG. 3.10. Lift the Sky Movement

> ## Cue
> Call out the A and B sections to guide movements and connect them with the musical form.

3. *We are going to play a movement game. Each of you will get a movement card, and there are two of each kind. Someone else in our class has the same card that you do. When the music starts, stand up and start performing the movement on your card, moving around the room. Keep an eye out for someone doing your movement to find your partner. You need to get to them before the **lyrics** "with a wink and a smile." Make sure to wink and smile at your partner on those words!*

> ## Cue
> Be sure to note the number of students in the class; if an odd number, the teacher needs to participate as a partner in the movement game.

4. Play the recording, and have students perform their movement and find their partner. Pause the recording at the end of the A section, after students have found partners.

5. *Next, we will create movements to perform during the B section. Think of one movement to perform or try a variety of movements to reflect the sound of this part of the music. After the B section, we will return to the A section, performing moves from the cards and finding partners.*

    Riff: Have students switch movement cards and repeat the game.

Grade 4

Fourth grade music is all about application.

Fourth grade learning focuses on expanded personal ownership of musical skills and knowledge and the ability to demonstrate individually and contribute to group music making. Musical experiences here should include a variety of activities that advance individual performance in addition to collaboration among classmates. At this level, students are able to begin individual instrument study; contribute to ensembles; create arrangements and accompaniments; perform stylized dances; read music notation of increasing complexity; and offer individual ideas to enhance collaborative music making.

Fundamentally, fourth grade music lessons include singing, playing, moving, listening, reading, creating, applying, and arranging—with the opportunity to demonstrate independent music making. They are emerging leaders who offer original expressions and contribute to the music learning experiences of others. Assessment should be individualized (formative and summative) and include opportunities for demonstration of skills/knowledge to happen alone and with others. In terms of jazz, students at this level are able to do things such as improvise individually with voices, instruments, and/or movement; trade fours with a partner; create personal interpretations; perform choreographed movements; and make choices based on personal preference and musical reasoning, for example.

At the fourth grade level, the jazz-based teaching strategies presented in this book will engage students to respond, create, and perform, in the following ways.

LEARNING OUTCOMES

Respond

- Demonstrate steady beat (macrobeat and/or microbeat).
- Employ non-locomotor and/or locomotor movement.
- Express ideas verbally.
- Express personal decisions with rationale.
- Express the feeling of a style of music.
- Imitate musical sounds and/or styles.
- Listen and describe music.
- Use instruments or singing voice to express ideas.

Create

- Arrange patterns and/or movements.
- Create an accompaniment.
- Create melodic patterns on instruments and/or with voices.
- Create personal interpretations.
- Create rhythmic patterns on instruments and/or with body percussion.
- Create scat/nonsense syllables.
- Explore new ways to use manipulatives in conjunction with music.
- Offer ideas for non-locomotor and/or locomotor movement.

Perform

- Perform body percussion.
- Perform chants, play-party games, stories, and/or poems with music.
- Perform dance and/or choreographed movement.
- Perform individually.
- Perform original non-locomotor and/or locomotor movement.
- Perform rhythmic patterns.
- Perform with a partner.
- Play classroom percussion instruments.
- Play, sing, and/or employ body percussion while reading rhythmic and/or melodic notation.
- Play soprano recorder.
- Sing songs, melodic patterns, and/or melodies.
- Use manipulative/prop to depict a musical idea.

4.1. Vocal Riffs and Scat: Scat Improvisations

Learning Outcomes

Respond:

- Express personal decisions with rationale.
- Imitate musical sounds and/or styles.

Create:

- Arrange patterns and/or movements.
- Create personal interpretations.
- Create scat/nonsense syllables.

Perform:

- Perform individually.
- Sing songs, melodic patterns, and/or melodies.

Learning Targets

✓Describe ✓Imitate ✓Listen ✓Sing

Music Selection

- "Basin Street Blues" Louis Armstrong (*Louis Armstrong Greatest Hits*, Sony Entertainment, Ltd., 1967)

Setup/Materials

- White boards, markers, erasers

Teaching Strategy

> **Cue**
>
> This scat improvisation is for the A section. The first phrase begins at 0:09.

1. Ask students to sing the **melody** of the **A section** using the neutral syllable "doo." *Jazz singers use nonsense syllables like "doo" to create* **scat solos**. *Now we will create our own* **scat syllables** *to perform with the song.*

2. Invite students to create a list of scat syllables, and write them on the board. *Select one or two of the scat syllables from our list to use in your scat.* Play the recording, and invite students to practice singing the melody with their selected syllables.

> **Cue**
>
> Encourage students to alternate between one or two syllables to ensure initial success with scat and gain confidence performing this jazz element.

3. Divide students into groups, and distribute white boards, markers, and erasers. Guide students to work together to replace "doo" using ideas listed on the board, and write them on their own white boards. Invite all groups at once to perform their original scats with the recording to practice.

4. **Take a Solo:** Select individual groups to stand and perform scat solos with an excerpt of the recording.

> **Cue**
>
> Place a check mark beside scat syllables used by groups to visually track selections on the board.

5. *Which scat syllables did we use most? Why do you think they were standouts?*

6. **Take a Solo:** Ask individual students to perform scat solos with the recording.

4.2. Brushing Up on Rhythm: Rhythms with Homemade Instruments

Learning Outcomes

Respond:

- Express the feeling of a style of music.
- Imitate musical sounds and/or styles.
- Use instruments or singing voice to express ideas.

Create:

- Create personal interpretations.
- Create rhythmic patterns on instruments and/or with body percussion.
- Explore new ways to use manipulatives in conjunction with music.

Perform:

- Perform rhythmic patterns.
- Perform with a partner.
- Play classroom percussion instruments.

Learning Targets

✓Improvise ✓Imitate ✓Lead ✓Listen ✓Play

Music Selection

- "Flute Salad" Oliver Nelson (*Jazz Flute*, U-5, 2015)

Setup/Materials

- Space for movement; drum brushes, envelopes, construction paper, markers, tape, scissors

 Set the Stage: Create a set of paper drum brushes of varying colors, papers, etc. to illustrate what the students will make (and have some on hand for students to use, if needed).

Teaching Strategy

1. *Let's listen to "Flute Salad" by Oliver Nelson and perform a variety of four-beat **"soft-shoe style"** rhythmic patterns. A soft-shoe style pattern sounds like a tap dancer dancing to jazz music.* Ask students to clap, tap a desk, or patsch as they imitate the following patterns and speak the phrase:

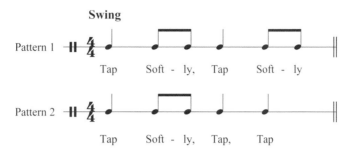

FIG. 4.2a. Tap Softly Rhythmic Anchor

2. **Take a Solo:** Demonstrate how to hold and play drum brushes, and select one student to play them by performing Pattern 1 or Pattern 2 for everyone to clap. Ask this student to select another student to become the leader and repeat.

> ## Cue
>
> Have students play drum brushes on a drum, cardboard box, or chair.

3. Invite students to find a partner and stand facing each other. *With your partner, you will **trade fours**, performing "soft-shoe style" rhythmic patterns like you are having a musical conversation. You may use Ta and Ta-di rhythms and continue to clap, tap a desk, patsch or identify other ways to perform your patterns.* Play the recording, and ask students to begin creating patterns.

4. *Now we are going to make our own drum brushes to play.* Distribute one envelope or piece of construction paper, markers, tape, and scissors to each student. Ask students to decorate their envelope or paper with the markers if they choose. Demonstrate how to make the instrument:

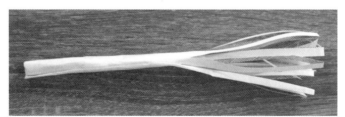

FIG. 4.2b. Homemade Drum Brush
[Photo by Michael Kipp]

   a. Cut "bristles" along the bottom edge of the envelope (approximately two inches long, ¼ inch wide).

   b. Roll envelope to create "brush handle" (with bristles at the bottom) and tape together.

5. Invite students to return to their partners and trade fours using their homemade drum brushes with the recording.

   Riff: Repeat with new partners.

4.3. Jammin' in C: Soprano Recorder Improvisations

Learning Outcomes

Respond:

- Demonstrate steady beat (macrobeat and/or microbeat).
- Listen and describe music.
- Use instruments or singing voice to express ideas.

Create:

- Create melodic patterns on instruments and/or with voices.
- Create personal interpretations.

Perform:

- Perform individually.
- Play, sing, and/or employ body percussion while reading rhythmic and/or melodic notation.
- Play soprano recorder.

Learning Targets

✓Connect ✓Describe ✓Improvise ✓Listen ✓Play ✓Read

Music Selection

- "C Jam Blues" Duke Ellington (*Blues in Orbit*, Columbia/Legacy, 1958)

Setup/Materials

- Sight-reading example; soprano recorders

Teaching Strategy

1. Display the sight-reading example, and invite students to perform it using their best music-reading skills and singing voices. *What rhythms do you see in the example?*

2. Distribute **soprano recorders**, or ask students to take out personal instruments. Remind students how to hold and play the recorders, and lead them to play the example on their instrument.

FIG. 4.3. Soprano Recorder Sight-Reading Example

> ## Cue
>
> Have students read through the rhythm first before adding pitches. Then, add soprano recorders to sequence the sight-reading process.

3. *Today, we are going to play along with a **12-bar blues** called "C Jam Blues," also known as "Duke's Place." This music was written by Duke Ellington and features the two notes that we played in our sight-reading example today, C and G. Play the recording, and have students perform the sight-reading example.*

4. Review the concept of **improvisation** with students. Play the recording, and ask students to play their recorders to improvise using C and G.

> ## Cue
>
> Asking students to freely improvise as a group while using limited pitches (C and G) provides structure and a safe space for free exploration and musical experimentation.

5. **Take a Solo:** Invite students to form a line in front of the class and improvise four-measure **solos** on their recorders using the two pitches (C and G). *You will step forward when it is your turn to perform and step back when you are finished. Feel free to use parts of our sight-reading example in your improvisation, but be sure to also add some original ideas!*

> ## Cue
>
> Students do not need to fill all four measures with pitches/sound. Teaching silence in improvisation is just as important as sound. Using **rests** and silences in solos can make them interesting.

4.4. High Fives in 5: Play-Party Game

Learning Outcomes

Respond:

- Demonstrate steady beat (macrobeat and/or microbeat).
- Employ non-locomotor and/or locomotor movement.
- Listen and describe music.

Create:

- Create personal interpretations.
- Offer ideas for non-locomotor and/or locomotor movement.

Perform:

- Perform body percussion.
- Perform with a partner.
- Play, sing, and/or employ body percussion while reading rhythmic and/or melodic notation.

Learning Targets

✓Describe ✓Listen ✓Move ✓Read

Music Selection

- "Take Five" The Dave Brubeck Quartet (*Time Out*, Columbia/Legacy, 1959)

Setup/Materials

- Space for movement; sight-reading example

> ### Cue
> Introduce the concept of **time signatures** and beat groups before this lesson.

Teaching Strategy

1. Display the sight-reading example on the board. Ask students to find the time signature, and lead a discussion about the number of **beats per measure** (five).

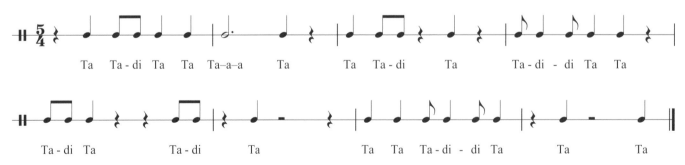

FIG. 4.4. Sight-Reading Example in 5/4

2. Ask students to read the example while speaking rhythm syllables and clapping.

3. **Take a Solo:** Select students to speak and clap the sight-reading example individually or with a partner.

4. *Today, we will be performing a play-party game to a song in 5/4.* Play the recording of "Take Five," and guide students to count and clap the beats per measure as they listen.

5. Ask students to perform the following **body percussion** pattern and label it as Pattern 1:

   Pattern 1:

Beats:	1	2	3	4	5
Body Percussion:	Patsch	Patsch	Patsch	Clap	Clap

6. Play the recording, and ask students to perform Pattern 1 with the track.

> ## Cue
> Encourage students to listen closely to match their movements to the beat groups 3 + 2.

7. Ask students to form partners and guide them to perform Pattern 2. *Now we will create hand movements using Patterns 1 and 2 in sequence.* Play the recording, and provide time for partners to practice.

   Pattern 2:

Beats:	1	2	3	4	5
Body Percussion:	Patsch	Patsch	Patsch	High Five	High Five

> ## Cue
> Have students "pump two hands to lift the sky" to replace the "two-hands high five" if you do not want students to physically connect.

8. *Now it's time for you and your partner to create your own hand movements. Remove the patsch, and replace it with a new movement. Be sure to fill three beats!*

9. **Take a Solo:** Select pairs to perform their play-party combination for the class.

4.5. Groovin' on the Sunny Side: Rhythm Instrument Improvisations

Learning Outcomes

Respond:

- Express personal decisions with rationale.
- Use instruments or singing voice to express ideas.

Create:

- Create personal interpretations.
- Create rhythmic patterns on instruments and/or with body percussion.

Perform:

- Perform chants, play-party games, stories, and/or poems with music.
- Perform individually.
- Play classroom percussion instruments.

Learning Targets

✓Describe ✓Improvise ✓Listen ✓Move ✓Play

Music and Chant Selections

- "On the Sunny Side of the Street" Sammy Nestico (*On the Sammy Side of the Street*, SN Publishing, 2012)
- "On the Sunny Side of the Street" Dizzy Gillespie, Sonny Rollins, Sonny Stitt (*50 Jazz Classics*, U-5 Reservoir Media Music, 2015)
- "Sunny Side with Jam" Darla S. Hanley

Setup/Materials

- Seated in a circle; variety of rhythm instuments on a music stand in the center of the circle

 Small cards with pictures and happy words to put in plastic egg containers (that open)

 Set the Stage: Print the set of cards, cut them to size, fold them, and place each one in a plastic egg for students to open and describe.

Teaching Strategy

1. Play the recording of "On the Sunny Side of the Street" (Sammy Nestico), and ask students to listen closely to be able to describe this music using their best music vocabulary.

2. *What does the phrase "on the sunny side of the street" mean to you?* Guide responses to ideas such as: warmth, bright and happy, flowers blooming, all good things.

3. *When jazz musicians get together, they sometimes do something called a **jam**. What do you think jam means in a jazz context?* Guide responses to musicians creating music together spontaneously, on the spot.

4. *Today, we are going to play a game called "Sunny Side with Jam." When your name is called, you move to the center and jam on one of the rhythm instruments on the music stand **improvising** rhythms to **accompany** the track. This is your opportunity to show your most musical performance, knowledge of how to hold and play the instruments, and to be creative on the spot—to improvise.*

5. Teach the "Sunny Side with Jam" chant by rote.

Sunny Side with Jam

Darla S. Hanley

Hard boiled, scrambled, baked or fried
Over easy
Sunny side

Toast or bagel
Hash brown yams
Calling [INSERT NAME] to the jam

Jammy, jammy
Jam, jam, jam
Calling [INSERT NAME] to the jam

Omelet, pickled, poached, or dyed
Over easy
Sunny side

6. **Take a Solo:** Ask students to stand, and select one student to go to the center. *The person in the center will improvise when we speak the "Jammy, Jammy, Jam, Jam, Jam" phrase. After you improvise you will choose someone to take your place in the center and the game will repeat. You will return to the circle and our new soloist improvises.*

> ### Cue
>
> Call the names of individuals, rather than have students select other students, to use these improvisations as an opportunity to assess specific students.

7. Play the recording, and direct students when to begin chanting. Continue the game until a majority (or all) of the students have had the opportunity to improvise/jam, as time permits.

   Riff: Create a movement pattern or body percussion sequence for students to perform in the outer circle throughout the game.

   Riff: Repeat using the Dizzy Gillespie recording. *Which "On the Sunny Side of the Street" did you prefer? Why?*

> ### Cue
>
> This Dizzy Gillespie track is primarily instrumental with a vocal beginning at 4:18. Note: He uses the lyrics, "Mmm wine" at 4:48. If preferred, use an excerpt of this recording to avoid that brief moment in the track.

4.6. The Swing Sick Strut: Dance with Partners

Learning Outcomes

Respond:

- Employ non-locomotor and/or locomotor movement.

Create:

- Offer ideas for non-locomotor and/or locomotor movement.

Perform:

- Perform dance and/or choreographed movement.
- Perform original non-locomotor and/or locomotor movement.
- Perform with a partner.

Learning Targets

✓Imitate ✓Listen ✓Move

Music Selection

- "High Hat, Trumpet, and Rhythm" Bria Skonberg (*With a Twist*, Okeh/Sony Masterworks, 2017)

Setup/Materials

- Space for movement

Teaching Strategy

1. Invite students to stand, and teach the following dance steps:

   March in Place (R, L, R, L)
   Jazz Square (R Foot cross in front of L, R, Together)
   Walk Forward (R, L, R, L)

   Double-Time Hand Pattern =
     R High Five to Partner
     Clap
     L High Five to Partner
     Clap
     Patsch, Patsch
     Clap

   Walk Backwards R, L, R, L

   Repeat Sequence

2. Ask students to form two lines facing each other and practice performing the dance movements.

> ## Cue
>
> Practice the hand pattern separately at a slow tempo to set students up for success in this part of the dance. Substitute a patsch, or two-hands high five pattern in place of hand pattern, if preferred.

3. Play the recording of "High Hat, Trumpet, and Rhythm," and invite students to perform the dance with the track (beginning at 0:04). *When you move forward, you will perform the hand pattern part of the dance with your partner. Be ready; this part is double time/fast.*

4. Guide students to change partners by adding a **groove** break as one line stays in place and the other line moves to the right to join and meet a new partner (with the student at the end walking all the way to the other end of the line to find their new partner).

> ## Cue
>
> Encourage students to explore a variety of movements as they groove and provide a verbal cue to inform them when to begin the dance.

 Riff: Have students perform this dance in a two-circle formation (i.e., form two circles with the inner circle facing a partner in the outer circle).

 Riff: Ask students to create a movement to replace marching each time it occurs in the dance.

4.7. Plates with Pizzazz: Dance

Learning Outcomes

Respond:

- Demonstrate steady beat (macrobeat and/or microbeat).
- Employ non-locomotor and/or locomotor movement.
- Express personal decisions with rationale.

Create:

- Create personal interpretations.
- Explore new ways to use manipulatives in conjunction with music.
- Offer ideas for non-locomotor and/or locomotor movement.

Perform:

- Perform original non-locomotor and/or locomotor movement.
- Perform with a partner.
- Use manipulative/prop to depict a musical idea.

Learning Targets

✓Describe ✓Listen ✓Move

Music Selection

- "In the Mood" Glenn Miller (*The Essential Glenn Miller*, RCA Victor/Legacy, 1996)

Setup/Materials

- Space for movement; paper plates

Teaching Strategy

> ### Cue
>
> This is designed to work with the first 1:09 of the recording. The A section begins at 0:11, and the B section at 0:46.

1. *Today, we will perform a dance with paper plates to "In the Mood" by Glenn Miller.*
2. Distribute plates (two per student), and teach the dance on the next page.
3. Guide students to form partners and perform the dance with the recording. *Tap your partner's plate to play the pattern following the circle walk.*
4. *Now you will be **choreographers** creating your own paper plate dance with your partner to perform with the recording. You may use the Ta, Ta-di, and Ta-a rhythms from our original routine as you create new movements. Your plate dance needs to be eight beats long.*
5. Demonstrate several plate movements for students to perform as examples including: clap, shake "jazzy hands," roller coasters, swim, patsch, move one at a time, hide behind the back, tap on hip, crisscross X. Play the recording, and provide time for students to create and practice.
6. **Take a Solo:** Invite pairs of students to perform their plate routines for the class.
7. *How did you choose your rhythms and plate movements?*

Cue

Asking students to reflect on decisions made to create original work that they like fosters a feeling of accomplishment and pride.

Introduction. Stand with plates together, and groove to the music.

A Section: 5x

Ta	-	di,	Ta	-	di,	Ta	-	di,	Ta
(Out		Clap	Out		Clap	Out		Clap	Clap)

Walk in a circle for four beats.

B Section: 3x

Ta	-	di,	Ta		Ta-a
(Tap		Tap	Tap		Shake)

Walk in a circle for four beats.

FIG. 4.7. Plates with Pizzazz Dance Sequence

4.8. Calling Time: Call-and-Response

Learning Outcomes

Respond:

- Demonstrate steady beat (macrobeat and/or microbeat).
- Imitate musical sounds and/or styles.
- Use instruments or singing voice to express ideas.

Create:

- Create personal interpretations.
- Create rhythmic patterns on instruments and/or with body percussion.

Perform:

- Perform individually.
- Play classroom percussion instruments.

Learning Targets

✓Lead ✓Listen ✓Play

Music and Chant Selections

- "Tico Tico" Paquito D'Rivera (*Spice it Up!*, Chesky Records, 2001)
- "It's Time!" Darla S. Hanley

Setup/Materials

- Tick-tocks, claves, wood blocks, rhythm sticks, bells, triangles, tambourines, shakers

 Set the Stage: Create an "It's Our Time for Music" bulletin board featuring pictures of students making music in class and/or in a school performance.

Teaching Strategy

1. *In music, we have something known as **call-and-response**. It's a way of making music together where someone says or does something—that's the call, and everyone responds with the same answer each time, which is the response. We are going to perform a clock-inspired call-and-response today.*

2. Ask students to clap and speak the response:

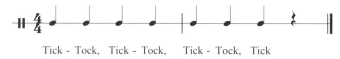

Tick - Tock, Tick - Tock,   Tick - Tock, Tick

FIG. 4.8a. Response

 3. **Take a Solo:** Invite everyone to stand, and select one student to play the **tick-tock** while the other students tap their toe to the right and left as they perform the response (moving their right foot like a car windshield wiper). Guide students to whisper "tick tock, tick tock" as they play or tap their toes.

4. *Next we will perform the call-and-response. Your response to the call is always the same (Tick-Tock, Tick-Tock, Tick-Tock, Tick, Rest).*

> ### Cues
>
> - Be ready to begin the call after a quick three-sixteenth-note pickup to ensure that the call-and-response aligns with the melodic form. The chant begins on the downbeat. This works best with the first 1:00 of the track.
> - The "It's Time!" chant is the call and the response is the "Tick-Tock" pattern shown in brackets each time.

5. Distribute **tick-tocks**, **claves**, **wood blocks**, **rhythm sticks**, etc. so that each student has an instrument.

6. Lead the call, and ask students to play the response on their instrument (first without the track to practice, then with the recording).

Riff: Distribute **bells**, **triangles**, **tambourines**, and **shakers**, and invite students to create a new response to imitate the sound of an alarm clock (e.g., Ring, Ring, Ring, Ring, R-i-i-ing, Rest = Ta, Ta, Ta, Ta, Ta-a-a, Rest).

Riff—Take a Solo: Use the phrase "time, time, it's time to play" as the call, and invite individual students to perform this call to prompt a response (either with **body percussion** or instruments).

It's Time!

Darla S. Hanley

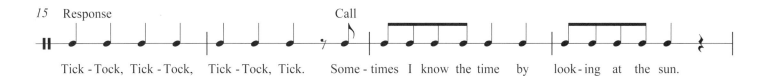

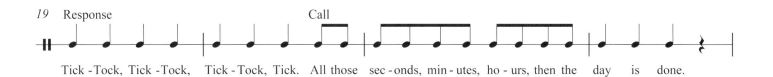

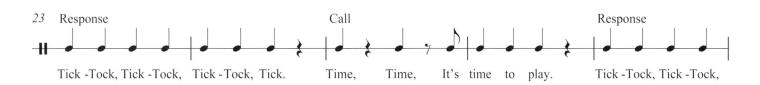

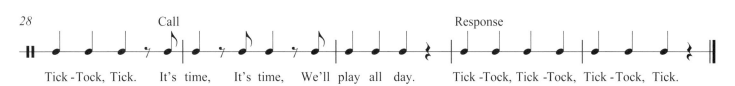

FIG. 4.8b. It's Time! Chant

4.9. Streets and Sounds: Body Percussion

Learning Outcomes

Respond:

- Demonstrate steady beat (macrobeat and/or microbeat).
- Employ non-locomotor and/or locomotor movement.
- Express ideas verbally.

Create:

- Create an accompaniment.
- Create personal interpretations.
- Create rhythmic patterns on instruments and/or with body percussion.

Perform:

- Perform body percussion.
- Perform individually.
- Perform rhythmic patterns.

Learning Targets

✓Compose ✓Describe ✓Listen ✓Move ✓Sing

Music Selections

- "On the Street Where You Live" the Four Freshmen (*Love Songs*, the Four Freshmen, 2012)
- "On the Street Where You Live" Alexis Cole, Bucky Pizzarelli (*A Beautiful Friendship*, Verve, 2015)

Setup/Materials

- Seated in a circle

Teaching Strategy

1. Teach students to sing "On the Street Where You Live" by rote.

> ### Cue
> Repeat the song as needed to set a foundation, as singing is an anchor to the **body percussion** accompaniment.

2. *Today, we will listen to a **vocal ensemble** called the Four Freshmen perform a song we know.* Play the recording, and ask students to listen for the familiar **melody**.

3. Teach the following body percussion accompaniment:

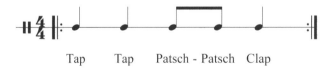

FIG. 4.9. Body Percussion Accompaniment

- Formation: Children seated (cross legged) on the floor with L palm facing up, R palm facing down (hovering over neighbor's palms).

> ### Cue
> L palm goes up to tap neighbor's palm while R palm goes down to tap neighbor's palm for each "Tap."

- Left hand moves up and right hand moves down, tapping neighbor's hands.

4. *This pattern will serve as an **accompaniment** and help us maintain a **steady beat**.* Have students perform the body percussion pattern with the track.

5. *Now we will **compose** four-beat-street patterns to the **instrumental interlude** and layer sounds to create a body percussion accompaniment. We will use an imaginary address to create rhythms. Take a few minutes to create an imaginary street name and house number, and the four-beat pattern that fits this address.*

Cues

- Use the street address for the school as an example, or a tree name (e.g., 7 Elm Street, 44 Pine Street).

- This game mimics a drum circle with individuals joining one-by-one until everyone is creating together. Providing time for students to explore personal ideas in advance will prepare them to join in turn and perform with success.

6. Invite one student to perform their repeating four-beat-street pattern. Add individual students in turn (creating and performing patterns) either around the circle or as selected until all are performing simultaneously. Repeat with the recording.

Cue

Use the instrumental interlude for the four-beat-street pattern improvisations. Note: it is thirty measures long (1:35 to 2:53). Depending on class size, divide students into multiple circles of ten to fifteen students to allow each student to perform their pattern at least twice.

7. Play the recording from the beginning and lead students to perform the accompaniment followed by the layered **improvisations** (ending at 2:53).

   Riff: Play the Alexis Cole and Bucky Pizzarelli recording, and invite students to perform the four-beat-street pattern accompaniment.

8. *How did you make your street name fit into four beats?*

4.10. Baseball Rhythms: Instrument Play

Learning Outcomes

Respond:

- Listen and describe music.
- Imitate musical sounds and/or styles.
- Use instruments or singing voice to express ideas.

Create:

- Create personal interpretations.
- Create rhythmic patterns on instruments and/or with body percussion.

Perform:

- Perform body percussion.
- Perform rhythmic patterns.
- Play, sing, and/or employ body percussion while reading rhythmic and/or melodic notation.

Learning Targets

✓Improvise ✓Listen ✓Move ✓Play ✓Read ✓Sing

Music Selections

- "Take Me Out to the Ball Game" Ray Brown Trio (*Three Dimensional*, Concord Records, 1992)

Setup/Materials

- Chromatic and diatonic boomwhackers, drumsticks

Teaching Strategy

1. Lead students to sing the traditional version of "Take Me Out to the Ball Game."

2. Play the recording of "Take Me Out to the Ball Game" by the Ray Brown Trio, and ask students to sing along when they hear the tune (melody begins at 0:13).

3. Display the traditional music notation (in the key of C) and have students read it and sing the piece.

> ## Cue
>
> "Take Me Out to the Ball Game" is available from many online sources and is public domain.

4. Guide students to clap and speak the following baseball rhythms.

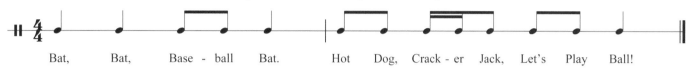

Bat,   Bat,   Base - ball Bat.   Hot Dog, Crack - er Jack, Let's Play Ball!

FIG. 4.10. Baseball Rhythms

5. Distribute instruments (one **boomwhacker** and two **drumsticks** per student).

> ## Cue
>
> Divide students into instrument groups if you do not have enough instruments for everyone to receive both boomwhackers and drumsticks.

 Riff: Substitute other non-pitched percussion for drumsticks to vary the learning experience.

6. Ask students to look closely at their boomwhacker to identify which pitch is represented. *We will play the song with our instruments as we read the music and sing. Be ready to play when your pitch comes in the song.*

> ## Cue
>
> Lead students to sing and play without the recording first to provide practice time before adding the track. The recording begins in the key of C and modulates to the key of A at 1:05. The baseball rhythms should be performed from 1:05 to 1:55.

7. Ask students to switch to drumsticks and practice playing the baseball rhythms. Start the recording at 1:05 and lead students to play the baseball rhythms with the track.

8. *Now we will put this all together so switch to your boomwhacker and prepare to sing, play instruments, and speak rhythms.* Play the recording, and guide students to begin.

9. *There is one more part to add to our music today! Let's listen to hear a question and answer exchange between the **bass** and **drums**.* Play the excerpt of the recording (1:56 to 2:34). *We will create our own drumstick **solos** every time we hear the drums. Listen to follow the bass each time and use your best musical ideas to create improvisations.*

10. Play the recording, and lead students to sing, play, speak, and improvise.

 Riff—Take a Solo: Invite students to create original baseball-themed rhythmic patterns. Select individual students to teach their patterns for everyone to play.

Grade 5

Fifth grade music is all about making personal musical connections.

Fifth grade learning focuses on personal ownership of musical skills and knowledge within specific contexts. Musical experiences here should include a variety of activities that engage students to perform individually, collaborate with classmates, and self-reflect while making musical connections. At this level, students are able to advance instrument study, contribute to the success of an ensemble, create arrangements and accompaniments, perform and create choreographed dances, read traditional notation of increasing complexity, and synthesize musical concepts as they make music.

Fundamentally, fifth grade music lessons include singing, playing, moving, listening, reading, creating, applying, arranging, and connecting—with opportunity for independent music making and musical choices based on personal preference. They are leaders who offer original expressions and contribute to the music learning experiences of others. Assessment should be individualized (formative and summative) and include opportunities for demonstrations of skills/knowledge to happen alone and with others. In terms of jazz, students at this level are able to do things such as improvise with voices, instruments and/or movement; use found sounds and manipulatives to express musical ideas; scat sing; use movement to show musical form; demonstrate stylistic nuance with voices, instruments, and/or movement; create and compare interpretations; use critical and creative thinking to make decisions and express preferences; combine musical concepts; and make connections based on prior learning, for example.

At the fifth grade level, the jazz-based teaching strategies presented in this book will engage students to respond, create, and perform, in the following ways.

LEARNING OUTCOMES

Respond

- Compare musical interpretations.
- Demonstrate pulse and meter.
- Employ non-locomotor and/or locomotor movement.
- Express personal decisions with rationale.
- Express personal preference with rationale.
- Explore uses of the voice to depict style, context, and/or personal interpretation.
- Follow aural cues.
- Listen and describe music.
- Move to reflect style of music.
- Use instruments or singing voice to express ideas.

Create

- Arrange patterns and/or movements.
- Create melodic patterns on instruments and/or with voices.
- Create personal interpretations.
- Create rhythmic patterns on instruments, manipulatives, and/or with body percussion.
- Explore new ways to use manipulatives in conjunction with music.
- Offer ideas for non-locomotor and/or locomotor movement.
- Offer ideas to create an original dance.

Perform

- Perform a composed accompaniment.
- Perform chants, play-party games, stories, and/or poems with music.
- Perform dance and/or choreographed movement.
- Perform individually.
- Play classroom percussion instruments.
- Play, sing, and/or employ body percussion while reading rhythmic and/or melodic notation.
- Sing songs a capella, with instrumental accompaniment, or with a recording.
- Use manipulative/prop to depict a musical idea.
- Use movements to depict a musical idea.

5.1. Announcing Jazz: Vocal Exploration

Learning Outcomes

Respond:

- Express personal decisions with rationale.
- Explore uses of the voice to depict style, context, and/or personal interpretation.

Create:

- Create personal interpretations.

Perform:

- Perform chants, play-party games, stories, and/or poems with music.
- Perform individually.

Learning Targets

✓Connect ✓Describe ✓Improvise ✓Listen

Music and Poetry Selections

- "Dave Brubeck, You'll Be Glad You Did" Darla S. Hanley
- "Besame Mucho" Dave Brubeck (*On Time*, SMSP, 2001)
- "When You Wish Upon a Star" the Dave Brubeck Quartet (*Dave Digs Disney (Legacy Edition)*, Columbia/Legacy, 1957)

Setup/Materials

- (Optional: microphone—real or prop)

Teaching Strategy

1. *Today, we will listen to a recording by Dave Brubeck and explore using our own voice to sound like an **announcer**.*

> ### Cue
> Lead a conversation about the role of announcers in the media to guide students, as needed.

2. Ask students to read the poem "Dave Brubeck, You'll Be Glad You Did" from the board (or projected on screen) with the recording and use their best "announcer" voice.

3. **Take a Solo:** Select individual students to read stanzas of the poem with the recording—changing their voice to be an announcer, to sound like jazz, to tell the story, etc.

Dave Brubeck, You'll Be Glad You Did
Darla S. Hanley

Calling all listeners
From near and from far
To hear cool jazz music
Wherever you are

With riffs, jumps, and swinging
This music is sweet
It's Brubeck's piano
That is such a treat

He dances with fingers
On keys black and white
So rhythmic and flowing
And always just right

Dave Brubeck the artist
Composer and more
An original jazzer
To know and adore

For Dave is a legend
A giant of jazz
Who shared lots of music
With flair and pizazz

"Blue Rondo," "Take Five," and
"Unsquare Dance" for sure
Are distinctive treasures
And art that endures

So calling all listeners
From grandmas to kids
To hear Brubeck's music
You'll be glad you did

> ### Cue
> If available, provide a **microphone** for students to use as they speak the poem with the track to inspire vocal exploration and make a real-world connection to technology used by announcers.

Riff: Repeat with the recording of Brubeck's "When You Wish Upon a Star." *How did you make your voice sound like an announcer? How did the different music change the way you spoke?*

> ### Cue
> This vocal exploration can happen with almost any Brubeck track. Varying music will influence and inspire students to use their voice in different ways, so multiple tracks are encouraged.

5.2. We ♥ Dance: Dance

Learning Outcomes

Respond:

- Employ non-locomotor and/or locomotor movement.
- Express personal decisions with rationale.
- Move to reflect style of music.

Create:

- Arrange patterns and/or movements.
- Create personal interpretations.
- Offer ideas to create an original dance.

Perform:

- Perform dance and/or choreographed movement.

Learning Targets

✓Arrange ✓Describe ✓Imitate ✓Move

Music Selection

- "Love Is a Simple Thing" Carmen McRae (*Carmen McRae: Finest Hour*, Verve, 2000)

Setup/Materials

- Space for movement

Teaching Strategy

1. Invite students to stand and teach the following dance steps (without the track). Play the recording of "Love Is a Simple Thing" by Carmen McRae, and practice performing the dance steps in sequence (Moves 1 to 4).

> ## Cue
> Movement begins at 0:14 following the introduction. All movements should consistently begin with the right or left direction (your choice). Move #4 is a single circle turn.

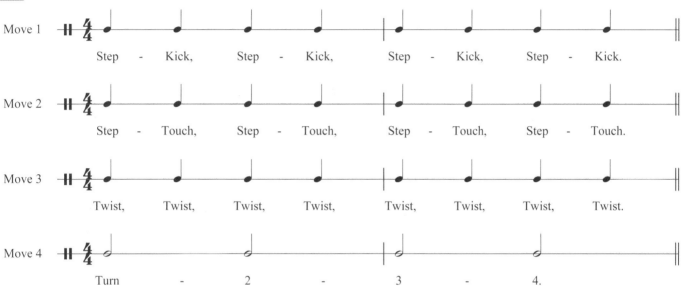

FIG. 5.2. Dance Steps in Four Moves

2. *Today, we will be **arrangers** and create our own dance using the four moves we just performed. As arrangers, you will decide the order of our dance steps.*

3. Identify a student to be the first arranger to choose one of the four movements and write the selection on the board (e.g., Move #__). Continue with other students to create an eight-measure dance sequence.

> ## Cue
> Students may select a dance move more than once in this sequence. This is an opportunity for student choice and expression.

4. Play the recording, and lead students to perform the new dance arrangement.

5. Invite students to turn to a neighbor and create an eight-beat dance move. Ask selected students to share their movements to create "Moves 5 to 8" to list on the board.

6. Invite student arrangers to create a new dance sequence using Moves 5 to 8 and perform this dance with the recording.

   Riff: Ask student arrangers to create a dance using Moves 1 to 8.

7. *What name would you give our dance? How does that name connect with the dance moves?*

5.3. Counting with Cups: Rhythmic Cup Game

Learning Outcomes

Respond:

- Compare musical interpretations.
- Demonstrate pulse and meter.
- Listen and describe music.

Create:

- Create personal interpretations.
- Explore new ways to use manipulatives in conjunction with music.

Perform:

- Perform a composed accompaniment.
- Use manipulative/prop to depict a musical idea.

Learning Targets

✓Describe ✓Imitate ✓Listen ✓Move

Music Selections

- "Unsquare Dance" the Dave Brubeck Quartet (*Time Further Out*, Legacy/Columbia, 1961)
- "Unsquare Dance" London Symphony Orchestra, arr. Chris Brubeck (*Dave Brubeck Live with LSO [feat. Darius Brubeck, Chris Brubeck…]*, LSO Live, 2001)

Setup/Materials

- Seated in a circle; plastic cups

 Set the Stage: Create a "Families Make Music" bulletin board featuring famous jazz musical families (e.g., Brubeck, Marsalis) with facts about their notable contributions.

Teaching Strategy

1. *Let's listen to music called "Unsquare Dance" by the Dave Brubeck Quartet. Listen closely to be ready to identify what **body percussion** you hear in the track.* (Clap)

2. Invite students to stand and teach the following body percussion **ostinato**:

Beats:	1	2	3	4	5	6	7
	Snap	Clap	Snap	Clap	Snap	Clap	Clap

> ## Cue
> Initially practice without the recording to provide opportunity for students to become familiar with the movements and **meter**.

3. Play the recording, and lead students to perform the ostinato with the track.

4. Ask students to speak the following rhythmic pattern with words:

FIG. 5.3. Rhythmic Pattern in 7/4

5. Distribute cups and transfer the rhythmic pattern to the cups.

> ## Cue
> Turn the cup over to create a surface on which to tap to begin the game. Guide students to whisper the words "pass the cup" (Ta, Ta, Ta) on the last measure as they pass cups to the person on their right.

6. Have students practice at their own pace without the recording. Play the recording, and guide students to play the pattern.

> ## Cue
> The **tempo** is fast. Use an app/tool to slow down the tempo to assist students as they learn the game if available.

Riff: Have students perform the cup routine to "Unsquare Dance," arranged by Chris Brubeck. *Which version of "Unsquare Dance" did you like best for the cup routine? Why?*

5.4. Ritzy Top Hats: Dance

Learning Outcomes

Respond:

- Demonstrate pulse and meter.
- Employ non-locomotor and/or locomotor movement.
- Move to reflect style of music.

Create:

- Create personal interpretations.
- Explore new ways to use manipulatives in conjunction with music.
- Offer ideas for non-locomotor and/or locomotor movement.

Perform:

- Perform dance and choreographed movement.
- Use manipulative/prop to depict a musical idea.

Learning Targets

✓Improvise ✓Listen ✓Move

Music Selection

- "Puttin' on the Ritz" Ella Fitzgerald (*Ella Fitzgerald Sings the Irving Berlin Song Book*, Verve, 1958)

Setup/Materials

 Space for movement; glitter top hats in several colors, color cards (one card per top hat color)

Teaching Strategy

> ### Cue
>
> For this top-hat routine, the pulse of "Puttin' on the Ritz" should be felt in half notes. The form of the song is **AABABA-Tag** with an instrumental interlude after the first **AABA**.

1. *Today, we will perform a top hat routine with Ella Fitzgerald's recording of "Puttin' on the Ritz."*
2. Invite students to stand, and distribute top hats (one per student).

 3. Ask students to place hats on the floor in front of them to begin, and teach the following sequence:

Introduction

- "Strut" walking around the hat (eight steps matching the half-note macrobeat).
- Pick up hat, twisting and turning it until for seven half-note macrobeat counts, placing it on head on count 8.

A Section Sequence

Continuing with half-note macrobeat pulse:

- Step-Kick, Step-Kick, Step-Kick, Step-Kick.
- R hand holds hat brim on each "step" and R arm extends to put hat in the air on each "kick."

Switch to quarter-note microbeat pulse:

- Step-Kick, Step-Kick, Step-Kick
- R hand holds hat brim on each "step" and R arm extends to put hat in the air on each "kick."
- Slide to the R with arms stretched (Fred Astaire dance move) on last phrase (ending with "ritz").

B Section Sequence

- Place hat in front of heart (top of hat away from body)
- Jazz Square (Step R, Cross L over R, Step Back R, Step Back L)
- Sway (R, L, R, L)
- Jazz Square (Step R, Cross L over R, Step Back R, Step Back L)
- Sway (R, L, R, L)

Tag (Final "Puttin' on the Ritz" Phrases)

- Slide to the L with arms stretched (Fred Astaire dance move) on last phrase (ending with "ritz").
- Place hat on the floor.
- "Strut" walking around the hat (eight steps matching the half-note macrobeat).
- Pick up hat, twisting and turning it placing it back on head to strike a pose to end the dance.

4. Play the recording, and have students practice parts for the **introduction** and **A and B sections**.

5. *During the **instrumental interlude** everyone is going to strike a "ritzy" pose and freeze until you see the color of your top hat on a color card. When you see your color, **improvise** movements with your hat until another color is shown. Return to your ritzy pose and the new dancers will improvise.*

> ## Cue
> Encourage students to use locomotor movements that show the style of the music and make use of top hats in creative ways.

 Riff—Take a Solo: Invite a student to call out color names and repeat the improvised movement section of the dance.

5.5. Benny's Bucket Band: Bucket Drums and Rhythms

Learning Outcomes

Respond:

- Demonstrate pulse and meter.
- Express personal decisions with rationale.
- Use instruments or singing voice to express ideas.

Create:

- Create personal interpretations.
- Create rhythmic patterns on instruments, manipulatives, and/or with body percussion.

Perform:

- Perform individually.
- Play classroom percussion instruments.
- Play, sing, and/or employ body percussion while reading rhythmic and/or melodic notation.

Learning Targets

✓Describe ✓Improvise ✓Lead ✓Listen ✓Play ✓Read

Music Selection

- "Sing, Sing, Sing" Benny Goodman (*The Essential Benny Goodman*, Columbia/Legacy, 2007)
- "Singing Bucket Rhythms" Allison P. Kipp

Setup/Materials

- Plastic five-gallon buckets, drumsticks

 Set the Stage: Create a "Found Sound Ensemble" bulletin board that features musical groups such as Stomp and the Recycled Orchestra of Cateura.

Teaching Strategy

> **Cue**
>
> This bucket band is designed to work with the first 1:59 of the recording.

1. *Today, we will play as an **ensemble** and perform in a bucket band!*

2. Distribute buckets (one per student) and **drumsticks** (two per student). Lead students in an echo-style warmup to play rhythmic patterns while exploring different **timbres** of the bucket drum (e.g., head, rim, sides, metal handle).

 3. **Take a Solo:** Invite students to speak, and play their name on their bucket drum following the question "Who's in the Band?" (Sycno-pa, Ta, Rest).

> **Cue**
>
> Lead students to play in a **call-and-response** manner and guide them to fit their name into four-beats using repetition and/or rests, as needed.

4. *Now we will perform with a big bang tune called "Sing, Sing, Sing" by Benny Goodman. Listen closely to hear the style and click your drumsticks together to play the beat.*

5. Ask students to read and play the "Singing Bucket Rhythms" piece on their bucket drums with drumsticks. *When we get to the **improvisation** section watch closely to know when it's your turn to play. Be sure to explore and use multiple parts of the bucket drum and your best rhythmic patterns in your improvised solos.*

Singing Bucket Rhythms

Allison P. Kipp

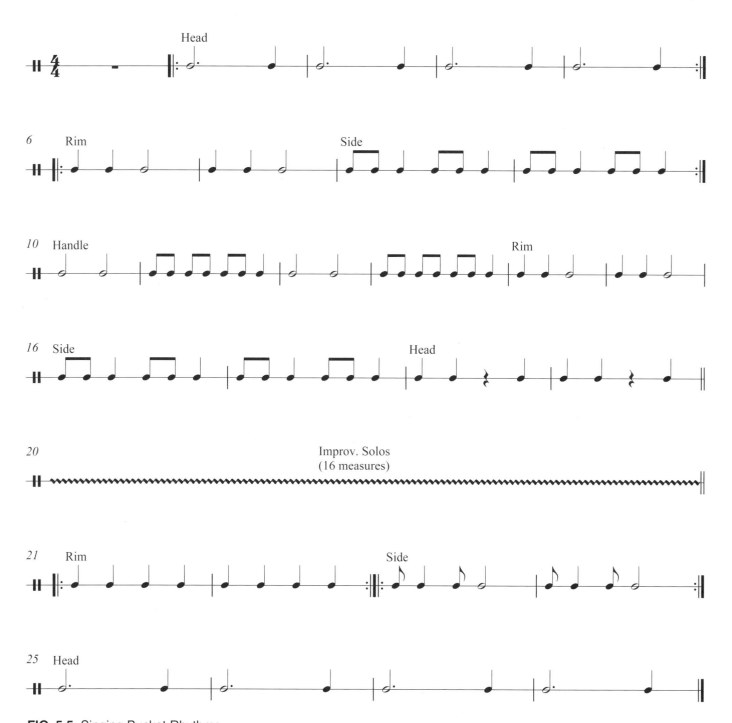

FIG. 5.5. Singing Bucket Rhythms

6. *Let's play our "Singing Bucket Rhythms" as a bucket drum ensemble with the recording. Remember to listen to each other so we all play the rhythms at the same time.*

7. *How did it feel to be part of the bucket ensemble? What decisions did you make as you played your improvisation (e.g., parts of the bucket, rhythms)?*

 Riff—Take a Solo: Invite individual students to be **conductors** to lead the band and point to select soloists to improvise.

5.6. Signing the Rainbow: Sign-Language Inspired Movement Improvisation

Learning Outcomes

Respond:

- Compare musical interpretations.
- Express personal decisions with rationale.
- Move to reflect style of music.

Create:

- Create personal interpretations.
- Explore new ways to use manipulatives in conjunction with music.

Perform:

- Sing songs a capella, with instrumental accompaniment, or with a recording.
- Use manipulative/prop to depict a musical idea.

Learning Targets

✓Connect ✓Describe ✓Improvise ✓Imitate ✓Lead ✓Listen ✓Move ✓Sing

Music Selections

- "I'm Always Chasing Rainbows" the Pied Pipers (*Capitol Collectors Series*, Capitol Records, 1992)
- "I'm Always Chasing Rainbows" Jo Stafford (*Broadway Revisited*, Corinthian Records, 2007)

Setup/Materials

- Space for movement; scarves; (optional: rainbow stretchy bands, parachutes)

Teaching Strategy

1. Teach students to sing "I'm Always Chasing Rainbows" by rote.
2. *Today, we will listen to a recording of the Pied Pipers (a **vocal group**) singing "I'm Always Chasing Rainbows." When singers sing together like this, they are part of an **ensemble**. Let's create our own ensemble and sing with the Pied Pipers.*
3. Play the recording, and lead students to sing.

4. Teach students to perform the **sign language** for the following colors of the rainbow:

RED: Place pointer finger on lower lip and flick finger down.

ORANGE: Start with closed fist under chin and open and close fist several times (like shaping an orange).

YELLOW: Form "Y" hand and quickly rotate wrist back and forth.

GREEN: Form "G" hand and quickly rotate wrist back and forth.

PURPLE: Form "P" hand and flick wrist twice away from body.

BLUE: Form "B" hand and quickly rotate wrist back and forth.

5. Play the **instrumental interlude** excerpt of the recording (1:40 to 2:03), and guide students to imitate the sign language while speaking each color.

6. Distribute scarves (one per student). *Now we will play a game. Listen closely and move your scarf to look like how the music sounds. You may move around the room or stay in place to improvise scarf moves but when you see the color of your scarf in sign language, stop in place and toss it in the air and catch it until another color is shown.*

7. Play the recording, and lead students to watch for sign language cues and perform with scarves.

   Riff: Ask individual students to perform sign language to lead the game.

8. *What decisions did you make to contribute to the success of our ensemble while singing with the recording of the Pied Pipers?*

   Riff: Play the Jo Stafford version of "I'm Always Chasing Rainbows," and use sign language to prompt movement exploration with rainbow stretchy bands, parachutes, or scarves tied together to create rainbows.

Cue

The slow tempo of this track provides an opportunity for sustained (non-stop) movements and stretched movement phrases that reflect the music. Use props to engage students to move slowly with discipline and self-control.

5.7. Pass the Percussion Please: Instrument Play

Learning Outcomes

Respond:

- Demonstrate pulse and meter.
- Follow aural cues.
- Use instruments or singing voice to express ideas.

Create:

- Create personal interpretations.
- Create rhythmic patterns on instruments, manipulatives, and/or with body percussion.

Perform:

- Perform individually.
- Play classroom percussion instruments.

Learning Targets

✓Describe ✓Improvise ✓Imitate ✓Listen ✓Move ✓Play

Music Selection

- "Hit That Jive Jack" Diana Krall (*All for You: A Dedication to The Nat King Cole Trio*, Impulse!, 1996)

Setup/Materials

- Seated in a circle; tambourines, maracas, egg shakers, (optional: music stand)

Teaching Strategy

1. Play the recording of "Hit That Jive Jack," and invite students to patsch and count (1-2-3-4) to demonstrate the macrobeat of the music.

2. Lead students to perform the following passing pattern:

	Take	Play	Play	Pass
Beats:	1	2	3	4

3. Distribute instruments to six students in the circle. *We are going to play a game where we all pass and play instruments around the circle to the beat of the music.*

> **Cue**
>
> Scatter instruments among students in the circle.

4. *Practice the following "Take/Play/Play/Pass" pattern using instruments:*

   Take: Students take the instrument from the person to the left of them.

   Play: Play on beat 2.

   Play: Play on beat 3.

   Pass: Pass to the person on the right.

Cue

Not all students will have instruments. Encourage everyone to speak the words "Take/Play/Play/ Pass" throughout. Ask those without instruments to patsch or tap the floor when they speak the word "play."

5. Play the recording, and invite students to begin passing and playing instruments. Passing begins at 0:09 and continues until the **instrumental interlude** (1:18).

6. *During the instrumental interlude, we will **improvise** on our instruments. Look around the room to identify the two people currently holding each type of instrument. Listen for the name of an instrument, and if you are the two students with that instrument, come to the center of the circle to have a musical conversation. Either person may begin, but just like in a speaking conversation, you need to wait until the person is finished to start playing (answering). You may create something new or **imitate** your partner. When the next instrument is called, give your instrument to someone who has not had a turn and return to the outside circle.*

Cues

- This musical conversation provides an opportunity for student leaders to emerge.
- Encourage students in the outside circle to maintain the macrobeat with body percussion while counting (1-2-3-4).

7. Play the recording beginning at 1:18, and lead students to perform musical conversations.

8. Invite students to put it all together to perform the passing game and musical conversations with the recording.

     Riff: Set rhythm instruments on a music stand in the center of the circle. Invite individual students to the center during the instrumental interlude to improvise eight-beat rhythmic patterns with the instrument(s) of their choice. Continue with multiple students in turn. Ask students in the outside circle to create original "Put It in Your Pocket" hand moves to perform until their name is called.

Cue

Using the phrase "Put It in Your Pocket" connects to lyrics and will inspire creativity. Encourage students to explore the use of simultaneous hands, alternating hands, single hand, etc. as they create movements.

9. *What words would you use to describe our "Pass the Percussion" game if you were having a conversation with a friend?*

5.8. Rhythm Relay: Instrument Relay Game

Learning Outcomes

Respond:

- Demonstrate pulse and meter.
- Move to reflect style of music.
- Use instruments or singing voice to express ideas.

Create:

- Create personal interpretations.
- Create rhythmic patterns on instruments, manipulatives, and/or with body percussion.

Perform:

- Play classroom percussion instruments.
- Play, sing, and/or employ body percussion while reading rhythmic and/or melodic notation.

Learning Targets

✓Arrange ✓Listen ✓Move ✓Play ✓Read

Music Selections

- "Sandu" Clifford Brown, Max Roach Quintet (*Study in Brown*, Verve Reissues, 1955)
- "Foxy" Buddy Rich (*The Argo, Verve & Emarcy Small Group Sessions*, Verve Reissues, 2011)

Setup/Materials

- Space for lines; hand drums; (optional: tambourines)

Teaching Strategy

1. *Let's listen to a recording of "Sandu" by Clifford Brown and the Max Roach Quintet. Keep the macrobeat as you listen. You may keep the beat any way you choose.*

2. Ask students to read and clap the following rhythmic patterns from the board:

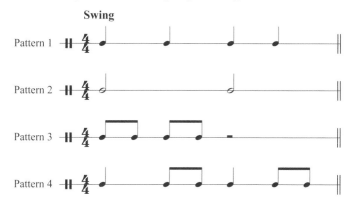

FIG. 5.8a. Rhythm Relay Rhythmic Patterns

3. Ask students to sit in three rows with everyone facing the board to create straight lines.

Board

X   X   X   X

X   X   X   X

X   X   X   X

X   X   X   X

X   X   X   X

X   X   X   X

FIG. 5.8b. Formation for Rhythm Relay

> ## Cue
>
> Rows facing the board provides an opportunity for students to reference the rhythmic patterns as they improvise, if needed.

4. Distribute a **hand drum** to the first person in each row. *Now we will perform a musical relay game. You will stand and play three of the rhythmic patterns on your instrument, pass the drum to the person behind you, and then sit down. You may **arrange** your three rhythmic patterns in any order. You will then have four beats to carefully pass the instrument. Instruments will move down the line with everyone standing, playing in turn, and when they reach the end the person in the back walks them to the front and the game repeats.*

5. Play the recording, and begin the game.

> ## Cue
>
> Having students sit to wait and stand to play allows them to clearly see the board and establishes them as soloists. Ask students to perform **body percussion** or **groove** to show the style and pulse of the music to keep them engaged while seated.

 Riff: Replace hand drums with tambourines, and perform the relay game.

 Riff: Perform the relay game with the recording of "Foxy" by Buddy Rich.

5.9. It's in the Bag: Movement Combinations

Learning Outcomes

Respond:

- Employ non-locomotor and/or locomotor movement.
- Express personal preference with rationale.
- Move to reflect style of music.

Create:

- Create personal interpretations.

Perform:

- Perform individually.
- Use movements to depict a musical idea.

Learning Targets

✓Describe ✓Improvise ✓Lead ✓Listen ✓Move

Music Selections

- "Bags' Groove: Take 1" Miles Davis (*Bags' Groove*, Prestige, 1987)
- "Bags' Groove" Oscar Peterson Trio (*Night Train – Expanded Edition*, Verve, 1963)

Setup/Materials

 Space for movement; two bags of movement directive cards

Teaching Strategy

1. Play the recording of "Bags' Groove" by Miles Davis, and ask students to move their head to show the **tempo** and **groove** of the music. Lead a discussion about tempo.

2. *Now we will play "What's in the Bag?" which is a multi-part movement game. One part tells us direction and the other tells us how and what to move. The secret instructions will be drawn from two bags. When you hear the descriptions, move around to room to show the tempo of the music using those elements.*

3. Draw the first directives (one per bag), play the recording, and begin the game.

BAG 1	BAG 2
Up and Down	Bouncing Shoulders
Diagonal	Bus Driver
Sideways	Chicken Elbows
Backwards	Dancing Feet
Forward	Drummer
	Music Teacher
	Old Man
	Piano Player
	Poppin' Knees
	Scrunchy Nose
	Sneaky Toes
	Trumpet Player
	Vibes Player
	Wagging Finger
	Wild Card Movement Freestyle

Cue

Walk around the room as students are moving and select individuals to choose a card and shout out the cue on the card to change the game.

4. *Now we will play the game to show the **style** of the music.* Play the recording, and begin the game.

   Riff: Select two students (one per bag) to draw directives and call them out following a cue from the teacher.

   Riff: Play the Oscar Peterson Trio version of "Bags' Groove," and repeat the game.

5. *Which music was best suited for your "Bus Driver" move? "Piano Player?" "Chicken Elbows?" How?*

5.10. Scatting to the Blues: Scat Improvisation

Learning Outcomes

Respond:

- Explore uses of the voice to depict style, context, and/or personal interpretation.
- Listen and describe music.
- Use instruments or singing voice to express ideas.

Create:

- Create melodic patterns on instruments and/or with voices.
- Create personal interpretations.

Perform:

- Perform individually.
- Play, sing, and/or employ body percussion while reading rhythmic and/or melodic notation.
- Sing songs a capella, with instrumental accompaniment, or with a recording.

Learning Targets

✓Connect ✓Describe ✓Improvise ✓Listen ✓Read ✓Sing

Music Selection

- "C Jam Blues" Duke Ellington (*Blues in Orbit*, Columbia/Legacy, 1958)

Setup/Materials

- Sight-reading example, white boards, markers, erasers

Teaching Strategy

1. *Think about a favorite food and how many syllables are in that word. Today, we will sing about our favorite foods using the pitches C and G.*

2. Display the sight-reading example, and lead students to read it using the pizza lyrics and their best singing voices.

I	like,	Oh,	yes I	like,	Piz -	za.
I	like,	Oh,	yes I	like,	Shu	Zat.
Shu	Dwee,	Bah,	Dit Du	Bop,	Skee	Bop.

FIG. 5.10. Sight-Reading Example

3. Play the recording of "C Jam Blues" by Duke Ellington, and invite students to sing the excerpt using the pizza lyrics with the track (entering after the first four measures).

4. Ask students to name food words with two syllables to replace the word "pizza." Play the recording, and sing with the new lyrics.

> ## Cue
>
> Vary this lyric writing by asking students to name healthy foods or foods in categories such as fruits.

5. *Next, we will perform a type of **vocal improvisation** called **scat**. We will replace the food word with **scat syllables**. Listen to the following scat pattern.* Ask students to look at the example and demonstrate the "I like, Oh, yes I like, Shu Zat" lyrics.

> ## Cue
>
> Asking students to listen as you sing provides an essential vocal model in their development as singers with the opportunity to hear scat syllables performed with jazz style.

6. Write the following scat syllables on the board, and ask students to select two to use in their scat (to replace "shu zat"):

Bah	Du	Skee
Bop	Dwee	Vee
Dit	Shu	Zat

7. Play the recording, and invite students to practice and improvise scat patterns.

 8. **Take a Solo:** Invite individual students to perform their scat with the recording.

9. *Now we will work with a partner and create a scat pattern. We will replace "I like, Oh, yes I like" each time with scat syllables. Be sure to match the scat syllables with the rhythm of the pattern. It may be helpful to sing as you make your choices.*

10. Ask students to find a partner; distribute whiteboards, markers, and erasers (one set per pair); and guide students to create scat patterns.

11. Play the recording, and ask students to practice their scat pattern.

12. **Take a Solo:** Invite three pairs of students to stand in a line in the front of the room. Play the recording, and have pairs perform their scats in turn to create a scat chain.

Index of Artists

This index includes the artists referenced in the teaching strategies by grade levels and page number.

APPENDIX B

Index of Chants and Poems

This index includes the original chants and poems referenced in the teaching strategies.

Overview of Learning Targets

GRADE K	TEACHING STRATEGY
Arrange	Red, Yellow, Blue: Color Arrangements, 16
Compose	
Connect	Lullaby My Jazzy Baby: Movement Exploration, 14 Red, Yellow, Blue: Color Arrangements, 16 Sounds Around Us: Word Chains, 20
Describe	Lullaby My Jazzy Baby: Movement Exploration, 14 Sounds Around Us: Word Chains, 20 Steady Ricky: Steady Beat, 4 Sweepy Moonbeams and Dancing Stars: Movement Exploration, 18 Tappin' Toes: Rhythmic Ostinato, 12
Improvise	Pass the Scat Hat: Scat Patterns, 10 Sweepy Moonbeams and Dancing Stars: Movement Exploration, 18
Imitate	Lullaby My Jazzy Baby: Movement Exploration, 14 Pass the Scat Hat: Scat Patterns, 10 Steady Ricky: Steady Beat, 4 Sweepy Moonbeams and Dancing Stars: Movement Exploration, 18 Tappin' Toes: Rhythmic Ostinato, 12
Lead	Red, Yellow, Blue: Color Arrangements, 16 Steady Ricky: Steady Beat, 4
Listen	Groovy Cat Moves/Scoobie Doobie Swim Moves: Movement Exploration, 3 Lullaby My Jazzy Baby: Movement Exploration, 14 Pass the Scat Hat: Scat Patterns, 10 Pretty Jazz Music to Dance With: Scarf Dance, 8 Red, Yellow, Blue: Color Arrangements, 16 Sounds Around Us: Word Chains, 20 Steady Ricky: Steady Beat, 4 Sweepy Moonbeams and Dancing Stars: Movement Exploration, 18 Tap It, Twist It, Wave: Movement with Partners, 6
Move	Groovy Cat Moves/Scoobie Doobie Swim Moves: Movement Exploration, 3 Lullaby My Jazzy Baby: Movement Exploration, 14 Pretty Jazz Music to Dance With: Scarf Dance, 8 Red, Yellow, Blue: Color Arrangements, 16 Sounds Around Us: Word Chains, 20 Sweepy Moonbeams and Dancing Stars: Movement Exploration, 18 Tap It, Twist It, Wave: Movement with Partners, 6 Tappin' Toes: Rhythmic Ostinato, 12
Play	Sounds Around Us: Word Chains, 20 Steady Ricky: Steady Beat, 4 Tappin' Toes: Rhythmic Ostinato, 12
Read	
Sing	Pass the Scat Hat: Scat Patterns, 10 Red, Yellow, Blue: Color Arrangements, 16 Tap It, Twist It, Wave: Movement with Partners, 6

GRADE 1	TEACHING STRATEGY
Arrange	Tea Cups for Two: Play Rhythms, 40
Compose	
Connect	The Alphabet: Like Do, Re, Mi—Sing and Chant, 36 Blue Skies and Happy Dances: Dance, 42 Hittin' the Town: Movement Exploration, 32 Painting with Scarves: Dance the Form, 34 Swinging Down the Railroad Tracks: Movement Imitation, 26
Describe	The Alphabet: Like Do, Re, Mi—Sing and Chant, 36 Blue Skies and Happy Dances: Dance, 42 Hittin' the Town: Movement Exploration, 32 Painting with Scarves: Dance the Form, 34 Ring the Bells: Instrument Sound/No Sound, 28 Swinging Down the Railroad Tracks: Movement Imitation, 26 We ♥ Jazz: Dance, 38
Improvise	The Alphabet: Like Do, Re, Mi—Sing and Chant, 36 Blue Skies and Happy Dances: Dance, 42 Hittin' the Town: Movement Exploration, 32 Jazzy Spider Charades: Movement Game, 30 Painting with Scarves: Dance the Form, 34 Ring the Bells: Instrument Sound/No Sound, 28
Imitate	Blue Skies and Happy Dances: Dance, 42 Ring the Bells: Instrument Sound/No Sound, 28 Swinging Down the Railroad Tracks: Movement Imitation, 26 We ♥ Jazz: Dance, 38
Lead	Blue Skies and Happy Dances: Dance, 42 Jazzy Spider Charades: Movement Game, 30 Swinging Down the Railroad Tracks: Movement Imitation, 26
Listen	The Alphabet: Like Do, Re, Mi—Sing and Chant, 36 Blue Skies and Happy Dances: Dance, 42 Hittin' the Town: Movement Exploration, 32 Jazzy Spider Charades: Movement Game, 30 Painting with Scarves: Dance the Form, 34 Ring the Bells: Instrument Sound/No Sound, 28 Swinging Down the Railroad Tracks: Movement Imitation, 26 Taking Turns with Rhythm: Instrument Play, 24 Tea Cups for Two: Play Rhythms, 40 We ♥ Jazz: Dance, 38
Move	The Alphabet: Like Do, Re, Mi—Sing and Chant, 36 Blue Skies and Happy Dances: Dance, 42 Hittin' the Town: Movement Exploration, 32 Jazzy Spider Charades: Movement Game, 30 Painting with Scarves: Dance the Form, 34 Ring the Bells: Instrument Sound/No Sound, 28 Swinging Down the Railroad Tracks: Movement Imitation, 26 Taking Turns with Rhythm: Instrument Play, 24 We ♥ Jazz: Dance, 38
Play	The Alphabet: Like Do, Re, Mi—Sing and Chant, 36 Ring the Bells: Instrument Sound/No Sound, 28 Taking Turns with Rhythm: Instrument Play, 24 Tea Cups for Two: Play Rhythms, 40
Read	Tea Cups for Two: Play Rhythms, 40
Sing	The Alphabet: Like Do, Re, Mi—Sing and Chant, 36 Jazzy Spider Charades: Movement Game, 30

GRADE 2	TEACHING STRATEGY
Arrange	Jazz Cats Scat: Scat Patterns, 52
Compose	Judge's Choice: Rhythmic Pattern Contest, 58
Connect	Jazz Cats Scat: Scat Patterns, 52 Rollin' and Steppin' to the Groove: Movement with Form, 60 Rondo Interpretations: Play the Form, 50
Describe	Jazz Takes a Walk: Improvised Movements, 56 Judge's Choice: Rhythmic Pattern Contest, 58 Pie Pan Partners: Dance, 62 Rondo Interpretations: Play the Form, 50 This Is Kathy's Waltz: Body Percussion, 46 Too Cool Conversations: Trade Solos, 48
Improvise	Jazz Takes a Walk: Improvised Movements, 56 Rhythm a Go-Go: Instrument Play, 54 Too Cool Conversations: Trade Solos, 48 We're Getting Fruity: Tambourine Improvisations, 64
Imitate	Jazz Cats Scat: Scat Patterns, 52 Jazz Takes a Walk: Improvised Movements, 56 Pie Pan Partners: Dance, 62 Rondo Interpretations: Play the Form, 50 This Is Kathy's Waltz: Body Percussion, 46
Lead	Pie Pan Partners: Dance, 62
Listen	Jazz Cats Scat: Scat Patterns, 52 Jazz Takes a Walk: Improvised Movements, 56 Judge's Choice: Rhythmic Pattern Contest, 58 Pie Pan Partners: Dance, 62 Rhythm a Go-Go: Instrument Play, 54 Rollin' and Steppin' to the Groove: Movement with Form, 60 Rondo Interpretations: Play the Form, 50 Too Cool Conversations: Trade Solos, 48 This Is Kathy's Waltz: Body Percussion, 46 We're Getting Fruity: Tambourine Improvisations, 64
Move	Jazz Cats Scat: Scat Patterns, 52 Jazz Takes a Walk: Improvised Movements, 56 Judge's Choice: Rhythmic Pattern Contest, 58 Pie Pan Partners: Dance, 62 Rhythm a Go-Go: Instrument Play, 54 Rollin' and Steppin' to the Groove: Movement with Form, 60 This Is Kathy's Waltz: Body Percussion, 46 Too Cool Conversations: Trade Solos, 48
Play	Judge's Choice: Rhythmic Pattern Contest, 58 Rhythm a Go-Go: Instrument Play, 54 Rondo Interpretations: Play the Form, 50 Too Cool Conversations: Trade Solos, 48 We're Getting Fruity: Tambourine Improvisations, 64
Read	Rhythm a Go-Go: Instrument Play, 54
Sing	

GRADE 3	TEACHING STRATEGY
Arrange	Drummers Meet Shakers: Instrument Groups, 80 USA States in Improv: Arranging Word Chains, 74
Compose	Dixieland Duos: Play-Party Game, 70 Drummers Meet Shakers: Instrument Groups, 80 USA States in Improv: Arranging Word Chains, 74
Connect	Finding Partners: Discover Movements, 86 Monk Moving Statues: Move and Freeze Dance, 72 Ready, Play, Switch: Instruments on Cue, 84 Rhumba Rhythms: Instrument Play, 76 USA States in Improv: Arranging Word Chains, 74
Describe	Dixieland Duos: Play-Party Game, 70 Drummers Meet Shakers: Instrument Groups, 80 Entrances and Exits: Improvised Movements, 82 Howdy Hay Dance: Dance, 78 Ready, Play, Switch: Instruments on Cue, 84 Rhumba Rhythms: Instrument Play, 76 USA States in Improv: Arranging Word Chains, 74
Improvise	Entrances and Exits: Improvised Movements, 82 Monk Moving Statues: Move and Freeze Dance, 72
Imitate	Dixieland Duos: Play-Party Game, 70 Howdy Hay Dance: Dance, 78 Ready, Play, Switch: Instruments on Cue, 84
Lead	Dixieland Duos: Play-Party Game, 70
Listen	Dixieland Duos: Play-Party Game, 70 Drummers Meet Shakers: Instrument Groups, 80 Entrances and Exits: Improvised Movements, 82 Everybody's Playin': Steady Beat and Melodic Rhythm, 68 Finding Partners: Discover Movements, 86 Howdy Hay Dance: Dance, 78 Monk Moving Statues: Move and Freeze Dance, 72 Ready, Play, Switch: Instruments on Cue, 84 Rhumba Rhythms: Instrument Play, 76 USA States in Improv: Arranging Word Chains, 74
Move	Dixieland Duos: Play-Party Game, 70 Entrances and Exits: Improvised Movements, 82 Everybody's Playin': Steady Beat and Melodic Rhythm, 68 Finding Partners: Discover Movements, 86 Howdy Hay Dance: Dance, 78 Monk Moving Statues: Move and Freeze Dance, 72 Ready, Play, Switch: Instruments on Cue, 84 USA States in Improv: Arranging Word Chains, 74
Play	Drummers Meet Shakers: Instrument Groups, 80 Entrances and Exits: Improvised Movements, 82 Everybody's Playin': Steady Beat and Melodic Rhythm, 68 Ready, Play, Switch: Instruments on Cue, 84 Rhumba Rhythms: Instrument Play, 76 USA States in Improv: Arranging Word Chains, 74
Read	Drummers Meet Shakers: Instrument Groups, 80 Rhumba Rhythms: Instrument Play, 76
Sing	

GRADE 4	TEACHING STRATEGY
Arrange	
Compose	Streets and Sounds: Body Percussion, 106
Connect	Jammin' in C: Soprano Recorder Improvisations, 94
Describe	Groovin' on the Sunny Side: Rhythm Instrument Improvisations, 98 High Fives in 5: Play-Party Game, 96 Jammin' in C: Soprano Recorder Improvisations, 94 Plates with Pizzazz: Dance, 102 Streets and Sounds: Body Percussion, 106 Vocal Riffs and Scat: Scat Improvisations, 90
Improvise	Baseball Rhythms: Instrument Play, 108 Brushing Up on Rhythm: Rhythms with Homemade Instruments, 92 Groovin' on the Sunny Side: Rhythm Instrument Improvisations, 98 Jammin' in C: Soprano Recorder Improvisations, 94
Imitate	Brushing Up on Rhythm: Rhythms with Homemade Instruments, 92 The Swing Sick Strut: Dance with Partners, 100 Vocal Riffs and Scat: Scat Improvisations, 90
Lead	Brushing Up on Rhythm: Rhythms with Homemade Instruments, 92 Calling Time: Call-and-Response, 104
Listen	Baseball Rhythms: Instrument Play, 108 Brushing Up on Rhythm: Rhythms with Homemade Instruments, 92 Calling Time: Call-and-Response, 104 Groovin' on the Sunny Side: Rhythm Instrument Improvisations, 98 High Fives in 5: Play-Party Game, 96 Jammin' in C: Soprano Recorder Improvisations, 94 Plates with Pizzazz: Dance, 102 Streets and Sounds: Body Percussion, 106 The Swing Sick Strut: Dance with Partners, 100 Vocal Riffs and Scat: Scat Improvisations, 90
Move	Baseball Rhythms: Instrument Play, 108 Groovin' on the Sunny Side: Rhythm Instrument Improvisations, 98 High Fives in 5: Play-Party Game, 96 Plates with Pizzazz: Dance, 102 Streets and Sounds: Body Percussion, 106 The Swing Sick Strut: Dance with Partners, 100
Play	Baseball Rhythms: Instrument Play, 108 Brushing Up on Rhythm: Rhythms with Homemade Instruments, 92 Calling Time: Call-and-Response, 104 Groovin' on the Sunny Side: Rhythm Instrument Improvisations, 98 Jammin' in C: Soprano Recorder Improvisations, 94
Read	Baseball Rhythms: Instrument Play, 108 High Fives in 5: Play-Party Game, 96 Jammin' in C: Soprano Recorder Improvisations, 94
Sing	Baseball Rhythms: Instrument Play, 108 Streets and Sounds: Body Percussion, 106 Vocal Riffs and Scat: Scat Improvisations, 90

GRADE 5	TEACHING STRATEGY
Arrange	Rhythm Relay: Instrument Relay Game, 126 We ♥ Dance: Dance, 114
Compose	
Connect	Announcing Jazz: Vocal Exploration, 112 Scatting to the Blues: Scat Improvisation, 130 Signing the Rainbow: Sign-Language Inspired Movement Improvisation, 122
Describe	Announcing Jazz: Vocal Exploration, 112 Benny's Bucket Band: Bucket Drums and Rhythms, 120 Counting with Cups: Rhythmic Cup Game, 116 It's in the Bag: Movement Combinations, 128 Pass the Percussion Please: Instrument Play, 124 Scatting to the Blues: Scat Improvisation, 130 Signing the Rainbow: Sign-Language Inspired Movement Improvisation, 122 We ♥ Dance: Dance, 114
Improvise	Announcing Jazz: Vocal Exploration, 112 Benny's Bucket Band: Bucket Drums and Rhythms, 120 It's in the Bag: Movement Combinations, 128 Pass the Percussion Please: Instrument Play, 124 Ritzy Top Hats: Dance, 118 Scatting to the Blues: Scat Improvisation, 130 Signing the Rainbow: Sign-Language Inspired Movement Improvisation, 122
Imitate	Counting with Cups: Rhythmic Cup Game, 116 Pass the Percussion Please: Instrument Play, 124 Signing the Rainbow: Sign-Language Inspired Movement Improvisation, 122 We ♥ Dance: Dance, 114
Lead	Benny's Bucket Band: Bucket Drums and Rhythms, 120 It's in the Bag: Movement Combinations, 128 Signing the Rainbow: Sign-Language Inspired Movement Improvisation, 122
Listen	Announcing Jazz: Vocal Exploration, 112 Benny's Bucket Band: Bucket Drums and Rhythms, 120 Counting with Cups: Rhythmic Cup Game, 116 It's in the Bag: Movement Combinations, 128 Pass the Percussion Please: Instrument Play, 124 Rhythm Relay: Instrument Relay Game, 126 Ritzy Top Hats: Dance, 118 Scatting to the Blues: Scat Improvisation, 130 Signing the Rainbow: Sign-Language Inspired Movement Improvisation, 122
Move	Counting with Cups: Rhythmic Cup Game, 116 It's in the Bag: Movement Combinations, 128 Pass the Percussion Please: Instrument Play, 124 Rhythm Relay: Instrument Relay Game, 126 Ritzy Top Hats: Dance, 118 Signing the Rainbow: Sign-Language Inspired Movement Improvisation, 122 We ♥ Dance: Dance, 114
Play	Benny's Bucket Band: Bucket Drums and Rhythms, 120 Pass the Percussion Please: Instrument Play, 124 Rhythm Relay: Instrument Relay Game, 126
Read	Benny's Bucket Band: Bucket Drums and Rhythms, 120 Rhythm Relay: Instrument Relay Game, 126 Scatting to the Blues: Scat Improvisation, 130
Sing	Scatting to the Blues: Scat Improvisation, 130 Signing the Rainbow: Sign-Language Inspired Movement Improvisation, 122

ABOUT THE AUTHORS

Dr. Darla S. Hanley

Dr. Darla S. Hanley, Dean of the Professional Education Division at Berklee College of Music, holds a PhD and MM in Music Education Research (Temple University) and a BM in Music Education and Vocal Performance (dual major) from the University of Massachusetts-Lowell. She is a member of Pi Kappa Lambda.

Darla is an experienced PK–12 music educator and arts leader who specializes in jazz and popular music education, creative movement, teacher education, and administration. Darla has experience with Warner Bros., Spotify, the Country Music Association, the Jazz Education Network, the Association for Popular Music Education, and NAfME, to mention a few examples.

Darla has presented sessions in nearly all 50 USA states and often works with teachers and students all over the world. Examples of some of her recent presentations and professional engagement include the International Congress for Education (Peru), Hong Kong Baptist University (Hong Kong), Viljandi Culture Academy and Tartu University (Estonia), Liceu Conservatory (Spain), and SXSW.edu Conference (Austin, TX). She is always seeking to find ways to advance music education.

Allison P. Kipp

Allison P. Kipp received both a BME and MME from Shenandoah Conservatory of Shenandoah University. She is an experienced music educator, private voice/piano teacher, adjudicator, and performer with 13+ years in the classroom.

Allison teaches at Legacy Elementary School in Loudoun County, Virginia where she guides the musical lives of hundreds of children in grades K–5 and within a self-contained K-2 Autism classroom. At Legacy, Allison started a chorus program, bucket band, and a recycled instrument and found-sound orchestra.

Allison is a member of NAfME, the Virginia Music Educators Association, the Jazz Education Network, and Sigma Alpha Iota. Examples of some of her recent presentations include sessions at the Massachusetts Music Educators Association Conference in Boston on the topics of musical creativity and performance for young children; and at the Jazz Education Network Conference in New Orleans on the topic of creative movement and improvisation in the elementary classroom.

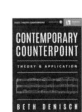